30 minute
ITALIAN

30minute
ITALIAN

contents

30 mins

All the recipes in this book can be prepared and cooked in under 30 minutes. Some recipes may require a little additional standing, cooling or refrigeration to reach perfection, but the hard work can be done in 30 minutes or less.

introduction

One thing all Italians have in common is their love of food, and especially their love of Italian food. Italian food is really based upon home cooking, 'mama's food', and it is in the homes that you will discover its true essence. It is the ritual of buying local ingredients in the market, sometimes twice a day for both lunch and dinner, and taking them home to cook that makes food an essential part of Italian life. Italians pick their ingredients carefully: if something isn't in season or doesn't look at its best on the market stall they'll choose to cook something else instead. There is a great saying that defines Italian food more than any other and that is 'the best meal is first prepared in the market'.

From Italy comes a wealth of definitive foods and flavours; who doesn't love the green, basil tang of pesto, adore the salty-sweet meatiness of prosciutto or could imagine life without the savoury smack of sun-dried tomatoes, parmesan cheese, salami, capers or anchovies? Perhaps Italian cooking is so popular because it is quietly sophisticated, bursting with flavour and relatively simple to make, especially in under 30 minutes. Sunny and laid-back like the inhabitants of her shores, the feel-good food of Italy is as worthy of an intimate sit-down dinner party as it is appropriate for a casual feast to be shared by a rowdy mob of family and friends.

Strictly speaking, though, it is a nonsense to talk of 'Italian food'. The respected food writer Claudia Roden goes so far as to exclaim, 'There is no such thing as Italian cooking. Only Sicilian, Piedmontese, Neopolitan, Venetian...and so on'. Italy is fiercely regional in its eating habits. The cookery of the north, traditionally rich in dairy products, meats, polenta and rice, is still quite distinct from that of the south, where tomato-based sauces, pasta, olive oil and fish conventionally hold sway. Whichever part of Italy a recipe or dish hails from though, it is bound to find favour at the table. Italian food never fails to please and, thankfully, isn't subject to the vagaries of faddism and fashion. From the perfect simplicity of insalata caprese and grilled sardines with basil and lemon, through to the baroque splendour of zucotto, zuppa inglese or zabaglione (and all the meat, fish and vegetables in between), no cook's repertoire is complete without an excellent collection of recipes from the beloved cucina Italiana.

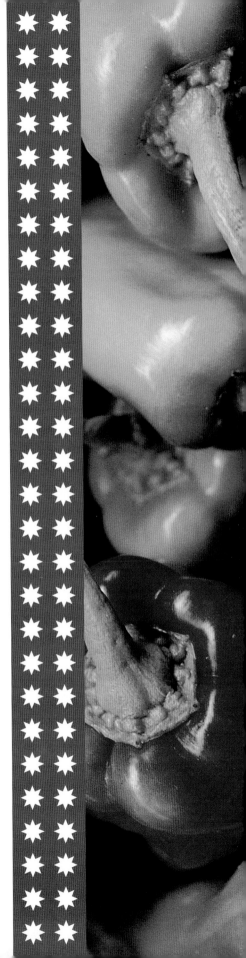

starters

Literally meaning 'before the meal' (pasto), and not 'before the pasta', as sometimes translated, antipasto can consist entirely of assorted vegetables, or can include meat, seafood and cheese. Bruschetta is a traditional Italian antipasto. Use slightly stale bread (this is an excellent dish for using up leftovers) that is dense enough to stop the olive oil seeping through. Technically speaking, real bruschetta is just plain grilled bread, rubbed with garlic while it is still hot and then drizzled with good-quality olive oil. For more great-tasting antipasto try the stuffed courgette flowers, king prawns with garlic, chilli and parsley, individual vegetable terrines with spicy tomato sauce, salmon carpaccio or the artichokes in aromatic vinaigrette.

The soups of Italy range from the hearty, warming, almost stew-like dishes of the north, like the zuppa di faggioli, thickened with beans, chestnuts or pearl barley, to the south's light vegetable-based soups such as the courgette pesto soup.

Fresh, good-quality vegetables feature prominently in Italian starters with several different preparation methods used for enhancing their flavour. Chargrilling or using a barbecue gives the vegetables a more complex taste than simply grilling them. The marks created by the griddle look attractive and have a smoky flavour that permeates the food.

Antipasto lends itself perfectly to relaxed entertaining and is so easy to prepare, with many recipes featured in this chapter requiring very little cooking. So follow the Italian example and buy the freshest ingredients possible, so you can enjoy these simple tasty starters.

12 mins

Bruschetta

SERVES: 8 ＊ **PREPARATION TIME: 10 MINUTES** ＊ **COOKING TIME: 1-2 MINUTES**

Bruschetta is a traditional Italian antipasto made using dense slightly stale bread that grills well. In its simplest form it is simply rubbed with garlic while still hot and then drizzled with extra virgin olive oil. For variations top with tomato, mushroom or aubergine.

4 plum (roma) tomatoes, chopped
80 ml (2½ fl oz/⅓ cup) olive oil
1 tablespoon balsamic vinegar
2 tablespoons chopped basil
8 slices day-old crusty Italian bread
1 garlic clove, peeled
chopped basil, to serve

1. Combine the tomatoes, olive oil, balsamic vinegar and chopped basil. Season well.

2. Toast the bread on one side. Rub the toasted side lightly with a peeled clove of garlic. Top with the tomato mixture and garnish with the extra chopped basil. Serve immediately.

basil

One of the most common herbs used in Italian cuisine, basil (basilico) adds a fresh flavour to cooked dishes and salads. It loses its flavour easily so add it at the end of cooking, tearing rather than chopping the leaves, to prevent the cut edges blackening.

Stuffed courgette flowers

MAKES: 20 ✳ **PREPARATION TIME: 15 MINUTES** ✳ **COOKING TIME: 15 MINUTES**

Courgette (zucchini) flowers can be found either attached to a stalk (male) or at the end of tiny courgettes (female). Before you use them, gently open out the flowers and check the insides to make sure there are no bugs.

75 g (2½ oz) plain (all-purpose) flour
100 g (3½ oz) mozzarella cheese
10 basil leaves
20 courgette (zucchini) flowers, stems and pistils removed
olive oil, for shallow-frying
2 lemon wedges, to serve

1. In a bowl, combine the flour with about 250 ml (1 cup) water, enough to obtain a creamy consistency. Add a pinch of salt and mix.

2. Cut the mozzarella cheese into 20 matchsticks. Insert a piece of mozzarella and some basil into each courgette flower. Gently press the petals closed.

3. Pour oil into a heavy-based frying pan to a depth of 2.5 cm (1 inch). Heat until a drop of batter sizzles when dropped in the oil.

4. Dip one flower at a time in the batter, shaking off the excess. Cook in batches for 3 minutes, or until crisp and golden. Drain on paper towels. Season and serve immediately with lemon wedges.

courgette flowers

Courgette flowers are one of the most delicious ways of eating vegetables. As their popularity increases, they have become easier to source, but if you can't find them at the supermarket, ask your local grocer. Male flowers have a stalk; the female ones have a baby courgette attached. Both are edible. Like all flowers, those from the courgette vine only last a few days after being picked, so make sure you buy them on the day you plan to use them.

30 mins

Minestrone

SERVES: 4 * **PREPARATION TIME: 15 MINUTES** * **COOKING TIME: 15 MINUTES**

Nearly every region in Italy has its own style of minestrone. Some add rice instead of pasta and others are finished with a spoonful of pesto, which is stirred through at the end. Minestrone should always be accompanied by plenty of freshly grated parmesan.

80 g (2¾ oz/½ cup) macaroni
1 tablespoon olive oil
1 leek, sliced
2 garlic cloves, crushed
1 carrot, sliced
1 waxy potato, chopped
1 courgette (zucchini), sliced
2 celery stalks, sliced
100 g (3½ oz) green beans, cut into
    short lengths
425 g (15 oz) tin chopped tomatoes
2 litres (70 fl oz/8 cups) vegetable
    stock
2 tablespoons tomato purée (paste)
425 g (15 oz) tin cannellini beans,
    rinsed and drained
2 tablespoons chopped flat-leaf
    (Italian) parsley
shaved Parmesan cheese, to serve

1. Bring a saucepan of water to the boil, add the macaroni and cook for 10-12 minutes, or until tender. Drain.

2. Meanwhile, heat the oil in a large heavy-based saucepan, add the leek and garlic and cook over medium heat for 3-4 minutes.

3. Add the carrot, potato, courgette, celery, green beans, tomato, stock and tomato purée. Bring to the boil, then reduce the heat and simmer for 10 minutes, or until the vegetables are tender.

4. Stir in the cooked pasta and cannellini beans and heat through. Spoon into warmed serving bowls and garnish with parsley and shaved parmesan.

parmesan

The making of Parmigiano Reggiano, the Italian hard cheese that is also simply known as parmesan, is strictly regulated. The cows can only be fed on grass and hay and the cheese is only made in certain areas of Emilia-Romagna such as Parma and Reggio Emilia. Each rind is marked with the place and date of making, as well as with the words Parmigiano Reggiano (look for this when buying Parmesan). Parmesan is traditionally not cut but broken into pieces with a special knife.

15 mins

King prawns with garlic, chilli and parsley

SERVES: 4 ∗ PREPARATION TIME: 10 MINUTES ∗ COOKING TIME: 5 MINUTES

There are many different types of prawn (gambero). Rather than judging by size, buy any that are fresh and in season – these will taste sweeter than frozen prawns, which are often woolly. Varieties of prawn are interchangeable in recipes: just ensure you have enough per person.

Cut the chilli in half. Cut out the membrane and scrape out any seeds. Cut off the stalk.

25 g (1 oz) butter
100 ml (3½ fl oz) olive oil
2 large garlic cloves, finely chopped
1 small red chilli, deseeded and finely chopped
16 king prawns (shrimp)
3 tablespoons chopped flat-leaf (Italian) parsley
lemon wedges, for serving

1. Heat the butter and oil together in a large frying pan and, when hot, add the garlic and chilli. Cook, stirring all the time, for 30 seconds. Add the prawns and cook for 3-4 minutes on each side, or until they turn pink.

2. Sprinkle the prawns with the parsley and serve immediately on hot plates with the lemon wedges to squeeze over them.

> **Note:** If you like you can heat up individual iron or stoneware dishes, transfer the just cooked prawns to them and serve the prawns still sizzling. Remember to provide finger bowls and napkins.

Lay each chilli half cut-side-down on the board and make cuts lengthways, reaching almost as far as the stalk end, then cut across the other way to give little squares.

30 mins

Individual vegetable terrines with spicy tomato sauce

SERVES: 4 ∗ PREPARATION TIME: 10 MINUTES ∗ COOKING TIME: 20 MINUTES

Ricotta means 'recooked'. It is a soft cheese made by recooking the whey left over from making other cheeses and draining it in baskets. It is produced as a by-product of many different types of cheese and varies in fat content. Fresh ricotta cut from a wheel has a better texture and flavour than that sold in tubs.

125 ml (4 fl oz/½ cup) oil
2 courgettes (zucchini), sliced on
   the diagonal
500 g (1 lb 2 oz) aubergines
   (eggplant), sliced
1 small fennel bulb, sliced
1 red onion, sliced
300 g (10½ oz) ricotta cheese
50 g (1¾ oz/½ cup) grated
   parmesan cheese
1 tablespoon chopped flat-leaf
   (Italian) parsley
1 tablespoon snipped chives
1 red and 1 yellow pepper
   (capsicum), grilled (broiled),
   peeled, cut into large pieces

Spicy tomato sauce
1 tablespoon oil
1 onion, finely chopped
2 garlic cloves, crushed
1 red chilli, seeded and chopped
425 g (15 oz) tin chopped tomatoes
2 tablespoons tomato purée (paste)

1. Heat 1 tablespoon of the oil in a large frying pan over high heat. Cook the courgette, aubergines, fennel and onion in batches for 5 minutes, or until golden, adding oil as needed. Drain separately on paper towels.

2. Preheat the oven to 200°C (400°F/ Gas 6). Mix together the ricotta, parmesan, parsley and chives. Season well.

3. Lightly grease and line four 315ml (1¼ cup) ramekins. Using half the aubergines, line the base of each dish. Continue layering with the courgette, pepper, cheese mixture, fennel and onion. Cover with the remaining aubergines and press down firmly. Bake for 10-15 minutes, or until hot. Leave for 5 minutes before turning out.

4. Meanwhile, to make the sauce, heat the oil in a saucepan and cook the onion and garlic for 2-3 minutes, or until soft. Add the chilli, chopped tomato and tomato purée and simmer for 5 minutes, or until thick and pulpy. Purée in a food processor. Return to the saucepan and keep warm. Spoon over the terrines.

20 mins

Salmon carpaccio

SERVES: 4 ＊ **PREPARATION TIME: 20 MINUTES** ＊ **COOKING TIME: NIL**

Carpaccio was created in the 1960's in Venice by the owner of Harry's Bar traditionally using beef. It is thought to have been named in honour of the Italian Renaissance painter, Vittore Carpaccio, whose use of reds is reflected in the colour of the dish.

3 vine-ripened tomatoes
1 tablespoon baby capers, rinsed
   and drained
1 tablespoon chopped dill
500 g (1 lb 2 oz) sashimi salmon
1 tablespoon extra virgin olive oil
1 tablespoon lime juice
ciabatta bread, to serve

1. Cut a cross in the base of the tomatoes. Place in a bowl and cover with boiling water. Leave to stand for 2-3 minutes, or until the skin blisters. Drain, plunge into cold water, then drain and peel. Cut the tomatoes in half, scoop out the seeds with a teaspoon and dice the flesh. Place in a bowl and stir in the capers and dill.

2. Using a very sharp knife, carefully slice the salmon into paper-thin slices, cutting across the grain. Divide the salmon equally among four plates, arranging in a single layer.

3. Place a mound of the tomato mixture in the centre of each plate. Whisk together the olive oil and lime juice, and season with salt. Drizzle over the tomato and salmon, and season with black pepper. Serve immediately with ciabatta bread.

Score a cross in the base of each tomato.

Plunge the tomato into cold water to stop further cooking. Peel the skin away from the cross and discard

Zuppa di faggioli

SERVES: 4 * **PREPARATION TIME: 10 MINUTES** * **COOKING TIME: 20 MINUTES**

This recipe is based on the authentic bean soup of Florence 'la ribollita'. If you like, spice it up by adding chopped chilli. Traditionally it is made a day in advance, then reboiled – 'ribollita'. It should be thick enough to eat with a fork rather than a spoon.

2 x 400 g (14 oz) tins cannellini
   beans
1 tablespoon extra virgin olive oil
1 leek, finely chopped
2 garlic cloves, crushed
1 teaspoon thyme leaves
2 celery stalks, diced
1 carrot, diced
1 kg (2 lb 4 oz) Swiss chard
   (silverbeet), trimmed and
   roughly chopped
1 ripe tomato, diced
1 litre (35 fl oz/4 cups) vegetable
   stock
2 small crusty rolls, each cut into
   4 slices
2 teaspoons balsamic vinegar
35 g (1¼ fl oz/⅓ cup) finely grated
   parmesan cheese

1. Put one tin of beans and liquid in a blender or small food processor and blend until smooth. Drain the other tin, reserving the beans and discarding the liquid.

2. Heat the oil in a large heavy-based saucepan, add the leek, garlic and thyme and cook for 2-3 minutes, or until soft and aromatic. Add the celery, carrot, Swiss chard and tomato and cook for a further 2-3 minutes, or until the Swiss chard has wilted. Meanwhile heat the stock in a separate saucepan.

3. Stir the puréed cannellini beans and stock into the vegetable mixture. Bring to the boil, then reduce the heat and simmer for 5-10 minutes, or until the vegetables are tender. Add the drained beans and stir until heated through. Season to taste with salt and cracked black pepper.

4. Arrange 2 slices of bread in the base of each soup bowl. Stir the balsamic vinegar into the soup and ladle over the bread. Serve topped with grated parmesan.

cannellini beans

Cream, almost white, beans which are usually used dried rather than fresh. They need to be soaked for a few hours to soften them before using them in recipes. Tinned beans can also be used—add them at the end of the cooking time or they will disintegrate.

10 mins

Insalata caprese

SERVES: 4 ✳ **PREPARATION TIME: 10 MINUTES** ✳ **COOKING TIME: NIL**

Insalata caprese is traditionally served with no other dressing than a drizzle of extra virgin olive oil to compliment the sharpness of the tomatoes. However, if you feel that your tomatoes may not have the best flavour, a little balsamic vinegar will help them along.

3 large vine-ripened tomatoes
250 g (9 oz) bocconcini (fresh baby
  mozzarella cheese)
12 basil leaves
60 ml (2 fl oz/¼ cup) extra virgin
  olive oil
4 basil leaves, roughly torn, extra

1. Slice the tomato into twelve 1cm (½ inch) slices. Slice the bocconcini into 24 slices the same thickness as the tomato.

2. Arrange the tomato slices on a plate, alternating them with two slices of bocconcini and placing a basil leaf between the bocconcini slices.

3. Drizzle with the olive oil, sprinkle with the torn basil and season well with salt and freshly ground black pepper.

> **Note:** You could use whole cherry tomatoes and toss them with the bocconcini and basil.

bocconcini

Means literally 'small mouthful' and is used to describe various foods, but generally refers to small balls of mozzarella, about the size of walnuts. True mozzarella is made from buffalo milk: that made from cow's milk is called fior di latte. The curds (mozzata) are stretched and shaped into balls by hand (though some balls are now factory made). Mozzarella should be white, fresh-smelling and have tiny holes that weep whey when it is very fresh.

25 mins

Individual Italian summer tarts

SERVES: 4 ∗ **PREPARATION TIME: 10 MINUTES** ∗ **COOKING TIME: 15 MINUTES**

Caramelised onion is very versatile and can be kept in the fridge for 1-2 weeks. Try serving it on a steak sandwich, in a cheese tart or on toast with melted gorgonzola.

80 g (2¾ oz/⅓ cup) caramelised red onion chutney
1 tablespoon chopped thyme
1 sheet ready-rolled puff pastry
170 g (6 oz) jar marinated quartered artichokes, drained
16 black olives, pitted
extra virgin olive oil, to serve
thyme sprigs, to garnish

1. Preheat the oven to 220°C (425°F/ Gas 7) and heat a lightly greased baking tray.

2. Stir the onion chutney and thyme together in a small bowl, until combined.

3. Cut four 10 cm (4 inch) rounds from the sheet of puff pastry and spread the onion chutney mixture over them, leaving a 1.5 cm (⅝ inch) border.

4. Place the pastry bases on the hot baking tray and cook in the top half of the oven for 12-15 minutes, or until the edges are risen and the pastry is golden brown.

5. Arrange the artichokes over the onion, then fill the spaces with olives. Drizzle the tarts with extra virgin olive oil and serve garnished with thyme.

black olives

Black olives are cured ripe olives. Like green olives, they can be brine-cured but as they are picked ripe they are less bitter than green and can also be salt-cured, or salt-cured then sun-dried. Choose the best quality olives you can afford and pit them yourself. Very black olives, which are sold pitted in cans, are often chemically cured dyed green olives.

16 mins

Grilled sardines with basil and lemon

SERVES: 4 ✳ PREPARATION TIME: 10 MINUTES ✳ COOKING TIME: 6 MINUTES

Small oily fleshed fish, sardines (sarde) can vary quite considerably in size. Different varieties of sardine are caught all over the world but some of the best are found in the Mediterranean. Sardines are best eaten very fresh as their flesh deteriorates quite quickly.

1 lemon, cut into thin slices
8 whole sardines, gutted, scaled
  and cleaned
coarse sea salt
80 ml (2½ fl oz/⅓ cup) olive oil
3 tablespoons torn basil leaves or
  whole small leaves

Fish substitution
Small herring, mackerel

1. Preheat the grill (broiler) or griddle to very hot. Insert a couple of slices of lemon inside each sardine and season on both sides with the sea salt and some freshly ground black pepper. Drizzle them with half of the olive oil.

2. Put the sardines on a baking tray and grill (broil) for 3 minutes on each side or place the fish directly onto the griddle. Check to see if the fish are cooked by lifting the top side and checking the inside of the fish. The flesh should look opaque. Remove and place in a shallow serving dish. Scatter the basil over the sardines and drizzle with the remaining olive oil. Serve warm or at room temperature.

sardines

Sleek, silver sardines belong to the herring family, which also includes anchovies. Sardines are fairly fatty, so they are ideal for barbecuing but they can also be marinated, baked, stuffed, smoked or tinned.

Prawn and bean salad

SERVES: 4 ✳ **PREPARATION TIME: 10 MINUTES** ✳ **COOKING TIME: 10 MINUTES**

Always remove the black thread-like vein, or intestinal tract, from prawns (shrimp) before cooking them. With practice, this will come away along with the head of the prawn when it is pulled off.

400 g (14 oz) tinned cannellini beans, drained and rinsed

8 slices chargrilled red peppers (capsicum)

300 g (10½ oz) green beans, trimmed

150 g (½ loaf) day-old ciabatta bread or other crusty loaf

80 ml (2½ fl oz/⅓ cup) olive oil

1 large garlic clove, finely chopped

1 kg (2 lb 4 oz) raw medium prawns, peeled and deveined, with tails intact

2 large handfuls flat-leaf (Italian) parsley

Dressing

60 ml (2 fl oz/¼ cup) lemon juice

60 ml (2 fl oz/¼ cup) olive oil

2 tablespoons capers, rinsed, drained and chopped

1 teaspoon sugar, optional

1. Place cannellini beans in a serving bowl. Cut pepper into strips, and add to the bowl.

2. Cook the green beans in a saucepan of boiling water for 3-4 minutes, or until tender. Drain and add to the serving bowl. Cut the bread into six slices, then cut each slice in four. Heat 60ml (2 fl oz/¼ cup) of the oil in a frying pan and cook the bread over medium heat on each side until golden. Remove from the pan.

3. Heat the remaining oil in the frying pan, add the garlic and prawns and cook for 1-2 minutes, or until the prawns are pink and cooked. Add to the salad with the parsley.

4. Combine the dressing ingredients, then season. Toss the dressing and bread through the salad.

30 mins

Artichokes in aromatic vinaigrette

SERVES: 4 ∗ **PREPARATION TIME: 10 MINUTES** ∗ **COOKING TIME: 20 MINUTES**

Artichokes are the edible flower of a member of the thistle family. The largest are usually boiled, but the smallest and most tender can be eaten raw as antipasto.

2 tablespoons lemon juice
4 large globe artichokes
2 garlic cloves, crushed
1 teaspoon finely chopped oregano
½ teaspoon ground cumin
½ teaspoon ground coriander
pinch dried chilli flakes
3 teaspoons sherry vinegar
60 ml (2 fl oz/¼ cup) olive oil

1. Add the lemon juice to a large bowl of cold water. Trim the artichokes, cutting off the stalks to within 5 cm (2 inches) of the base and removing the tough outer leaves. Cut the top quarter of the leaves from each. Slice each artichoke in half from top to base, or into quarters if large. Remove each small, furry choke with a teaspoon, then put the artichokes in the bowl of acidulated water to prevent them from discolouring while you prepare the rest.

2. Bring a large non-reactive saucepan of water to the boil, add the artichokes and a teaspoon of salt and simmer for 20 minutes, or until tender. The cooking time will depend on the artichoke size. Test by pressing a skewer into the base. If cooked, the artichoke will be soft and give little resistance. Strain, then place the artichokes on their cut side to drain.

3. Meanwhile combine the garlic, oregano, cumin, coriander and chilli flakes in a bowl. Season, and blend in the vinegar. Beating constantly, slowly pour in the oil to form an emulsion. This can be done in a small processor.

4. Arrange the artichokes in rows on a platter. Pour the vinaigrette over the top and leave to cool completely.

Snap off the tough outer leaves until you reach the paler tender ones.

Cut away the top quarter of the globes, dropping them into lemon water when completed.

30 mins

Courgette pesto soup

SERVES: 4 ∗ PREPARATION TIME: 10 MINUTES ∗ COOKING TIME: 20 MINUTES

Zucchini is the Italian name for courgettes. Varieties include the common dark green ones, pale green ones known as 'white' and yellow ones. Some are long and thin, others are ball-shaped. Tiny 'baby' courgettes are also available as are their flowers.

1 tablespoon olive oil
1 large onion, finely chopped
2 garlic cloves, crushed
750 ml (26 fl oz/3 cups) vegetable or chicken stock
750 g (1 lb 10 oz) courgettes (zucchini), thinly sliced
60 ml (2 fl oz/¼ cup) cream
toasted ciabatta bread, to serve

Pesto
2 large handfuls basil
25 g (¼ cup) finely grated parmesan cheese
2 tablespoons pine nuts, toasted
2 tablespoons extra virgin olive oil

1. Heat the olive oil in a large heavy-based saucepan. Add the onion and garlic and cook over medium heat for 3-4 minutes, or until the onion is soft.

2. Meanwhile bring the stock to the boil in a separate saucepan. Add the courgette and hot stock to the onion mixture. Bring to the boil, then reduce the heat, cover and simmer for about 10 minutes, or until the courgette is very soft.

3. To make the pesto, process the basil, parmesan and pine nuts in a food processor for 20 seconds, or until finely chopped. Gradually add the olive oil and process until smooth. Spoon into a small bowl.

4. Transfer the courgette mixture to a blender or food processor and blend in batches until smooth. Return the mixture to the pan, stir in the cream and 2 tablespoons of the pesto, and reheat over medium heat until hot. Season with salt and black pepper and serve with toasted ciabatta bread. Serve the remaining pesto in a bowl for diners to help themselves, or cover with olive oil and store in the refrigerator for up to 1 week.

Tuna and white bean salad

SERVES: 4-6 ✻ **PREPARATION TIME: 15 MINUTES** ✻ **COOKING TIME: 5 MINUTES**

Tuna (tonno) is a large fish with oily flesh that can be used as steaks, pieces of fillet or cut into cubes. It grills well as it is fairly robust and holds its own with strong flavours like lemon and tomato.

400 g (14 oz) tuna steaks
1 small red onion, thinly sliced
1 tomato, seeded and chopped
1 small red pepper (capsicum),
    thinly sliced
2 x 400 g (14 oz) tins cannellini
    beans
2 garlic cloves, crushed
1 teaspoon chopped thyme
4 tablespoons finely chopped flat-
    leaf (Italian) parsley
1½ tablespoons lemon juice
80 ml (2½ fl oz/⅓ cup) extra virgin
    olive oil
1 teaspoon honey
olive oil, for brushing
100 g (3½ oz) rocket (arugula)
1 teaspoon lemon zest

1. Place the tuna steaks on a plate, sprinkle with cracked black pepper on both sides, cover with plastic and refrigerate until needed.

2. Combine the onion, tomato and pepper in a large bowl. Rinse the cannellini beans under cold running water for 30 seconds, drain and add to the bowl with the garlic, thyme and 3 tablespoons of the parsley.

3. Place the lemon juice, oil and honey in a small saucepan, bring to the boil, then simmer, stirring, for 1 minute, or until the honey dissolves. Remove from the heat.

4. Brush a barbecue or chargrill with olive oil, and heat until very hot. Cook the tuna for 1 minute on each side. The meat should still be pink in the middle. Slice into 3 cm (1¼ inch) cubes and combine with the salad. Pour on the warm dressing and toss well.

5. Place the rocket on a platter. Top with the salad, season and garnish with the zest and remaining parsley.

tuna

There are many varieties of tuna, all of which are interchangeable in recipes though the colour of the flesh may vary. Tuna is caught off the coast of Sicily in huge tunnels of nets: a practice peculiar to the region.

pasta, risotto & gnocchi

Italy's most famous export, pasta, comes in every shape and size under the hot Mediterranean sun. In the fiery south, dried pasta is dressed with chillies and tomatoes, the hallmark of that region's history of cucina povera (poor kitchen). Rich Emilia-Romagna is known for its many varieties of fresh golden egg pasta, simply dressed with butter or shaved truffles. The fame of Italy's pasta sauces – primavera, carbonara, basil pesto and Bologna's meat ragú – has now spread far beyond the country's borders.

For dried pasta 75g (2¾ oz) provides a small portion, 125g (4½ oz) a main course and 150g (5¼ oz) a large portion. If you are using fresh pasta the weights will be slightly less (the moisture contents of the fresh pasta means that it weighs more per portion).

Pasta has to be cooked in lots of rapidly boiling salted water – about 1 litre (33 fl oz) of water and 1 teaspoon salt per 100g (3½ oz) (of pasta.
The pan must be large enough for the pasta to move freely. It is not necessary to add oil to the cooking water or the draining pasta; all this does is coat the pasta and encourage the sauce to slide off. When you drain pasta, don't do it too thoroughly – a little water left clinging to the pasta will help the sauce spread through it.

Pasta sauces vary from thin butter or oil dressing flavoured with garlic, chilli or herbs to robust stew-like sauces of meat or vegetables. Sauces in Italy are applied sparingly: the pasta is the main ingredient and the sauce an addition. Parmesan is often served alongside, but in Italy it would not be offered with sauces containing fish, shellfish or chilli.

Risotto is often referred to as the pasta of the north. The famous creamy arborio rice from Lombardy's Po Valley, is flavoured and coloured with saffron, vegetables and squid ink and served thick or liquid enough to eat from a spoon, depending on where in Italy you are dining.

There are three well-known varieties of risotto rice that are widely available today. Arborio rice which produces a stickier risotto, Vialone nano which gives a looser consistency but keeps more of the bite in the middle and finally Carnaroli which makes a creamier risotto, but with a firm consistency.

The texture of risotto varies throughout northern Italy. Milanese risottos are much stiffer than those of Venice, which are served all'onda, meaning 'like waves'. You can make a risotto to any consistency you like. For a wetter risotto, add a tablespoon or two of hot stock right at the end, just before you serve.

The recipes that follow show how simple flavours like pancetta, cream and egg or basil, pine nuts and parmesan can make delicious quick meals.

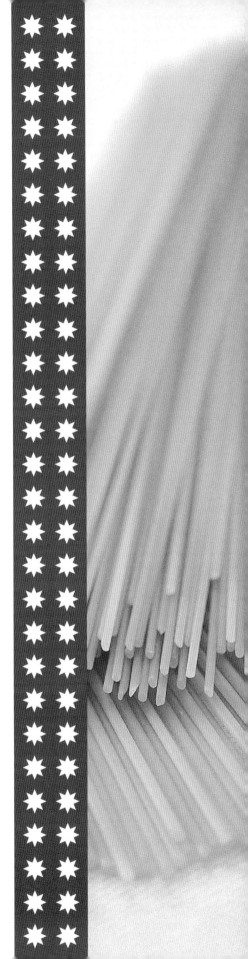

15 mins

Spaghetti carbonara

SERVES: 4 * **PREPARATION TIME: 5 MINUTES** * **COOKING TIME: 10 MINUTES**

The rich Roman pasta dish is classically made with guanciale, which is the cured meat made from the salted, air-dried cheeks of pigs, with pancetta being a good substitute. The raw egg yolks are cooked by the heat of the pasta, which is stirred into the sauce just before serving. Carbonara is usually served with spaghetti or bucatini.

1 tablespoon olive oil
300 g (10½ oz) pancetta, cut into
  small dice
160 ml (5½ fl oz/⅔ cup) double
  (thick/heavy) cream
6 egg yolks
400 g (14 oz) spaghetti
65 g (2¼ oz/⅔ cup) grated
  parmesan cheese

1. Heat the olive oil in a saucepan and cook the pancetta for 5 minutes, stirring frequently, until it is light brown and crisp. Tip the pancetta into a sieve to strain off any excess oil.

2. Mix the cream and egg yolks together in a bowl, and when the pancetta has cooled, add it to the egg mixture.

3. Meanwhile cook the spaghetti in a large saucepan of boiling water, according to packet instruction, until *al dente,* stirring once or twice to make sure the pieces are not stuck together. Drain the spaghetti and reserve a small cup of the cooking water.

4. Put the spaghetti back in the saucepan and put it over a low heat. Add the egg mixture and half the parmesan, then take the pan off the heat, otherwise the egg will scramble. Season with salt and pepper and mix together. If the sauce is too thick and the pasta is stuck together, add a little of the reserved cooking water. The spaghetti should look as if it has a fine coating of egg and cream all over it.

5. Serve the spaghetti in warm bowls with more parmesan sprinkled over the top.

pancetta

Coming from the Italian word pancia which means belly, pancetta is exactly the same cut of meat as bacon but it is not smoked. There are two types of pancetta: pancetta stesa, a flat type which is cured for about three weeks and then hung to air and dry for up to four months, and pancetta arrotolata, which is rolled into a salami-like shape. In the Italian kitchen, pancetta stesa is used to flavour sauces, stews and pastas, and the rolled pancetta is mainly used as part of an antipasto platter.

30 mins

Mushroom risotto

SERVES: 4 * **PREPARATION TIME: 5 MINUTES** * **COOKING TIME: 25 MINUTES**

This delicious classic risotto is often made using dried porcini, which have a wonderful earthy flavour. The porcini are soaked in water to soften them and then the soaking water is added to the stock so that none of the flavour is wasted.

1.5 litres (52 fl oz/6 cups) vegetable
  stock
500 ml (17 fl oz/2 cups) white wine
2 tablespoons olive oil
60 g (2¼ oz) butter
1 leek, thinly sliced
500 g (1 lb 2 oz) flat mushrooms,
  sliced
500 g (1 lb 2 oz/2¼ cups) arborio
  rice
75 g (2½ oz/¾ cup) grated
  parmesan cheese
3 tablespoons chopped flat-leaf
  (Italian) parsley
balsamic vinegar, to serve
shaved Parmesan cheese, to
  garnish
flat-leaf (Italian) parsley, to garnish

1. Place the stock and wine in a large saucepan, bring to the boil, then reduce the heat to low, cover and keep at a low simmer.

2. Heat the oil and butter in a large saucepan. Add the leek and mushrooms and cook over medium heat for 3-4 minutes, or until soft and tender. Stir in the arborio rice until it is translucent.

3. Add 125 ml (4 fl oz/½ cup) stock, stirring constantly over medium heat until the liquid is absorbed. Continue adding more stock, 125ml (4 fl oz/½ cup) at a time, stirring constantly for 20 minutes, or until all the stock is absorbed and the rice is tender and creamy.

4. Stir in the parmesan and chopped parsley until all the cheese is melted. Serve drizzled with vinegar and top with parmesan shavings and parsley.

Stir frequently to ensure all the grains are coated evenly.

Add the liquid a ladleful at a time.

27 mins

Baked sweet potato and watercress gnocchi

SERVES: 6 ＊ **PREPARATION TIME: 20 MINUTES** ＊ **COOKING TIME: 7 MINUTES**

Dust your hands well with flour before rolling the gnocchi because the mixture can be very sticky. Roll the gnocchi into walnut-sized balls. These may seem larger than gnocchi you usually see, but traditional sizes vary all over Italy. If you try to make them smaller, they will not hold together very well.

700 g (1 lb 9 oz) cooked, orange
   sweet potato
300 g (10½ oz) cooked desiree
   potatoes
350 g (12 oz) plain (all-purpose)
   flour
35g (1¼ oz/⅓ cup) grated
   parmesan cheese
30g (1 oz/1 cup) watercress leaves,
   finely chopped
1 garlic clove, crushed
60 g (2¼ oz) butter
25 g (1 oz/¼ cup) grated Parmesan
   cheese, extra
2 tablespoons chopped parsley

1. Peel the cooked sweet potato and desiree potatoes and press through a potato ricer or mouli into a bowl. Add the flour, grated parmesan, watercress and garlic, and season well. Gently bring together with your hands until a soft dough forms. It is important not to overwork the dough to keep the gnocchi tender. Portion into walnut-size pieces and shape using the back of a fork to create the traditional 'gnocchi' shape.

2. Melt the butter in a large roasting tray. Preheat the grill (broiler) to medium-high heat.

3. Cook the gnocchi in a large saucepan of boiling salted water for 2 minutes, or until they rise to the surface. Scoop out with a slotted spoon, draining the water off well. Arrange in the roasting tray, tossing gently in the butter, and grill for 5 minutes, or until lightly golden. Sprinkle with the extra parmesan and chopped parsley and serve immediately.

Use a fork to make deep ridges.

Pasta with tomato and basil sauce

SERVES: 4 ✶ **PREPARATION TIME: 10 MINUTES** ✶ **COOKING TIME: 15 MINUTES**

Basil (basilico) is one of the most common herbs used in Italian cuisine, and adds a fresh flavour to cooked dishes and salads. It loses its flavour easily so add it at the end of cooking, tearing rather than chopping the leaves, to prevent the cut edges blackening.

500 g (1 lb 2 oz) penne rigate
80 ml (2½ fl oz/⅓ cup) extra virgin olive oil
4 garlic cloves, crushed
4 anchovy fillets, finely chopped
2 small red chillies, seeded and finely chopped
6 large, vine-ripened tomatoes, peeled, seeded and diced
80 ml (2½ fl oz/⅓ cup) white wine
1 tablespoon tomato purée (paste)
2 teaspoons sugar
2 tablespoons finely chopped flat-leaf (Italian) parsley
3 tablespoons shredded basil

1. Cook the pasta in a saucepan of boiling salted water until *al dente*. Drain well.

2. Meanwhile, heat the oil in a frying pan and cook the garlic for 30 seconds. Stir in the anchovy and chilli and cook for a further 30 seconds. Add the tomato and cook for 2 minutes over high heat. Add the wine, tomato purée and sugar and simmer, covered, for 10 minutes, or until thickened.

3. Toss the tomato sauce through the pasta with the herbs. Season and serve with grated parmesan, if desired.

parsley

There are two main types of parsley (prezzemolo) used in Italian cooking. Flat-leaf, or Italian, parsley is used to add flavour to dishes, while curly parsley, with its tightly furled leaves, is relegated mainly to use as a garnish.

22 mins

Genovese pesto sauce

SERVES: 4 * **PREPARATION TIME: 15 MINUTES** * **COOKING TIME: 7 MINUTES**

Traditionally, pesto sauce is served with trennette pasta, green beans and potatoes but you can leave out the vegetables if you prefer or use spaghetti. Pesto is traditionally made in a mortar and pestle but a food processor also works well.

Pesto
2 garlic cloves
50 g (1¾ oz) pine nuts
3 large handfuls basil, stems removed
150-180 ml (5-6 fl oz) extra virgin olive oil
50 g (1¾ oz) parmesan cheese, finely grated, plus extra to serve

500 g (1 lb 2 oz) trennette
175 g (6 oz) green beans, trimmed
175 g (6 oz) small potatoes, very thinly sliced

1. Put the garlic and pine nuts in a mortar and pestle or food processor and pound or process until finely ground. Add the basil and then drizzle in the olive oil a little at a time while pounding or processing. When you have a thick purée stop adding the oil. Season and mix in the parmesan.

2. Bring a large saucepan of salted water to the boil. Add the pasta, green beans and potatoes, stirring well to prevent the pasta from sticking together. Cook until the pasta is *al dente* (the vegetables should be cooked by this time), then drain, reserving a little of the water.

3. Return the pasta and vegetables to the saucepan, add the pesto, and mix well. If necessary, add some of the reserved water to loosen the pasta. Season and serve immediately with extra parmesan.

pesto

This famous Italian sauce goes especially well with pasta or fish. It requires a little patience when adding the oil which must be drizzled very slowly and gradually into the basil and pine nut mixture. Pesto should always be used raw at room temperature and never warmed up.

30 mins

Spaghetti with meatballs

SERVES: 4 ✳ **PREPARATION TIME: 10 MINUTES** ✳ **COOKING TIME: 20 MINUTES**

Meaning 'little strings', spaghetti is made all over Italy, originally in lengths of up to 50 cm (20 inches). It is eaten with a variety of sauces, often those containing oil, such as the simple garlic and oil sauce (aglio e olio). Spaghetti is sold in a variety of thickness including a thinner version, spaghettini.

Meatballs
500 g (1 lb 2 oz) minced (ground) beef
40 g (1½ oz/½ cup) fresh breadcrumbs
1 onion, finely chopped
2 garlic cloves, crushed
2 teaspoons Worcestershire sauce
1 teaspoon dried oregano
30 g (1 oz/¼ cup) plain (all-purpose) flour
2 tablespoons olive oil

Sauce
1 tablespoon olive oil
1 onion, finely chopped
2 garlic cloves, crushed
2 x 400 g (14 oz) tins chopped tomatoes
2 tablespoons tomato purée (paste)
125 ml (4 fl oz/½ cup) beef stock
2 teaspoons sugar

500 g (1 lb 2 oz) spaghetti
grated parmesan cheese, optional

1. Combine the mince, breadcrumbs, onion, garlic, Worcestershire sauce and oregano in a bowl and season to taste. Use your hands to mix the ingredients together well. Roll level tablespoons of the mixture into balls, dust lightly with the flour and shake off the excess. Heat the oil in a deep frying pan and cook the meatballs in batches, turning frequently, until browned all over. Drain well.

2. Meanwhile to make the sauce, heat the oil in a large deep frying pan. Add the onion and cook over medium heat for a few minutes until soft and just lightly golden. Add the garlic and cook for 1 minute more. Add the tomatoes, tomato purée, stock and sugar to the pan and stir to combine. Bring the mixture to the boil, and add the meatballs. Reduce the heat and simmer for 15 minutes, turning the meatballs once. Season with salt and pepper.

3. Meanwhile, cook the spaghetti in a large pan of boiling water until just tender. Drain, divide among serving plates and top with the meatballs and sauce. Serve with grated parmesan if desired.

Saffron prawn risotto

SERVES: 4 ✳ **PREPARATION TIME: 5 MINUTES** ✳ **COOKING TIME: 25 MINUTES**

It is often pointed out that saffron *(zafferano)* is one of the most expensive commodities in the world, and is literally worth more than its own weight in gold. However, it is so light and so little is usually needed that it is not an expensive item to buy.

¼ teaspoon saffron threads
60 ml (2 fl oz/¼ cup) olive oil
2 garlic cloves, crushed
3 tablespoons chopped parsley
500 g (1 lb 2 oz) prawns (shrimp), peeled and deveined, tails intact
60 ml (2 fl oz/¼ cup) dry sherry
60 ml (2 fl oz/¼ cup) white wine
1.5 litres (52 fl oz/6 cups) hot fish stock
1 onion, chopped
440 g (15½ oz/2 cups) risotto rice

1. Soak the saffron threads in 60ml (2 fl oz/¼ cup) hot water.

2. Heat half the oil in a saucepan. Add the garlic, parsley and prawns and season with salt and pepper. Cook for 2 minutes, then add the sherry, wine and saffron with the liquid. Remove the prawns with a slotted spoon and set aside. Simmer until the liquid has reduced by half. Pour in the stock and 250 ml (9 fl oz/1 cup) water, cover and keep at a constant simmer.

3. Meanwhile in a separate large heavy-based saucepan, heat the remaining oil. Cook the onion for 3 minutes, or until golden. Add the rice and stir over medium heat for 3 minutes.

4. Add 125 ml (4 fl oz/½ cup) stock, stirring constantly over medium heat until the liquid is absorbed. Continue adding more stock, 125 ml (4 fl oz/½ cup) at a time, stirring constantly for 20 minutes, or until all the stock is absorbed and the rice is tender and creamy. Add the prawns and stir until heated through. Season, then serve.

saffron

Saffron can be bought in small packets or as a ground powder (the whole stigmas are preferable). Cheaper saffron is inferior in aroma and flavour. The most important thing to remember when using saffron is that it is very strong and can be overpowering, so don't be tempted to use more than the recipe specifies.

20 mins

Orecchiette with broccoli

SERVES: 6 * **PREPARATION TIME: 5 MINUTES** * **COOKING TIME: 15 MINUTES**

Orecchiette, meaning 'little ears' is usually associated with Puglia. The shape is made by pressing the thumb onto small discs of pasta dough that are then left to dry. The resulting indentation 'traps' the sauce, which is often vegetable based.

750 g (1 lb 10 oz) broccoli, cut into florets
450 g (1 lb) orecchiette
60 ml (2 fl oz/¼ cup) extra virgin olive oil
½ teaspoon dried chilli flakes
30 g (1 oz/⅓ cup) grated pecorino or parmesan cheese

1. Blanch the broccoli in a saucepan of boiling salted water for 5 minutes, or until just tender. Remove with a slotted spoon, drain well and return the water to the boil. Cook the pasta in the boiling water until *al dente*, then drain well and return to the pan.

2. Meanwhile, heat the oil in a heavy-based frying pan and add the chilli flakes and broccoli. Increase the heat to medium and cook, stirring for 5 minutes, or until the broccoli is well coated and beginning to break apart. Season. Add to the pasta, toss in the cheese and serve.

Spaghetti vongole

SERVES: 4 * **PREPARATION TIME: 10 MINUTES** * **COOKING TIME: 20 MINUTES**

Vongole is Italian for clams, and there are many species to choose from. When preparing to cook, check to make sure all the clams are alive by tapping any open ones on the side of the sink. If they do not close, discard them.

2 tablespoons olive oil
3 garlic cloves, crushed
2 pinches of chilli flakes
125 ml (4 fl oz/½ cup) dry white wine
400 g (14 oz) tin chopped tomatoes
3 tablespoons finely chopped flat-leaf (Italian) parsley
1 kg (2 lb 4 oz) clams (vongole), cleaned
400 g (14 oz) spaghetti or linguine
½ teaspoon grated lemon zest
lemon wedges, for serving

1. Heat the oil in a large deep frying pan. Add the garlic and chilli and cook over low heat for 30 seconds. Add the white wine, tomatoes and 1 teaspoon of the parsley. Increase the heat and boil, stirring occasionally, for 8-10 minutes, or until the liquid is reduced by half.

2. Add the clams to the pan and cover with a lid. Increase the heat and cook for 3-5 minutes, or until the clams open, shaking the pan often. Remove the clams from the pan, discarding any that stay closed. Stir in the remaining parsley and season. Boil the sauce for 3-4 minutes until it is thick. Set half the clams aside and extract the meat from the rest.

3. Meanwhile, cook the pasta in a large saucepan of boiling salted water until *al dente*. Drain and stir through the sauce. Add the lemon zest, reserved clams and clam meat and toss well. Serve with the lemon wedges.

clams

Clams are bivalve molluscs, and are classed as either soft or hard-shelled. Hard-shelled clams come in different sizes and colours, and all are good raw or cooked. Soft-shelled clams, which have brittle shells that gape open, are most common in North America. Clams must be bought live, then cleaned and shucked just before use.

30 mins

Pasta with squash and feta

SERVES: 4 ∗ **PREPARATION TIME: 10 MINUTES** ∗ **COOKING TIME: 20 MINUTES**

Squash *(zucca)* is used in both savoury and sweet dishes in Italy. The name zucca actually means 'all squash' so varieties often have their own names. Squash is used to fill pasta or as a sauce, baked as a vegetable, put in soups, candied or used in breads and cakes.

1 kg (2 lb 4 oz) butternut squash (pumpkin), peeled and cut into 2 cm (¾ inch) chunks
1 red onion, thinly sliced
8 garlic cloves, unpeeled
1 tablespoon rosemary leaves
80 ml (2 fl oz/⅓ cup) olive oil
400 g (14 oz) casserechi pasta, or macaroni, gemelli or other short pasta
200 g (7 oz) marinated feta cheese, crumbled
2 tablespoons grated parmesan cheese
2 tablespoons finely chopped parsley

Preheat the oven to 200°C (400°F/ Gas 6). Put the squash, onion, garlic and rosemary in a roasting tin, then drizzle with 1 tablespoon (½ fl oz) of the oil. Season. Using your hands, rub the oil over all the ingredients until well coated. Roast for 20 minutes, or until the squash is soft and starting to caramelise.

1. Meanwhile, cook the pasta in a saucepan of boiling salted water until *al dente*.

2. Squeeze the roasted garlic out of its skin and place it in a bowl with the remaining oil. Mash with a fork.

3. Add the garlic oil to the hot pasta, then the remaining ingredients. Toss well and season.

feta cheese
Feta is traditionally made using sheep or goat's milk but these days milk from cows is more often used. Feta cheese is made in large blocks and cured and stored in brine.
It develops a salty rich flavour and quite a crumbly texture.

30 mins

Spaghetti puttanesca

SERVES: 4 ＊ **PREPARATION TIME: 15 MINUTES** ＊ **COOKING TIME: 15 MINUTES**

Although versions of this robust, piquant sauce are now made all over Italy, puttanesca is usually associated with Naples and Calabria. This dish is never served with cheese but often sprinkled with fresh parsley just before serving.

400 g (14 oz) spaghetti
2 tablespoons olive oil
1 onion, finely chopped
2 garlic cloves, finely sliced
1 small red chilli, cored, seeded and sliced
6 anchovy fillets, finely chopped
400 g (14 oz) tin chopped tomatoes
1 tablespoon fresh oregano, finely chopped
16 black olives, halved and pitted
2 tablespoons baby capers
1 handful basil leaves

1. Cook the spaghetti in a large saucepan of boiling salted water until *al dente,* stirring once or twice to make sure the pieces are not stuck together. The cooking time will vary depending on the brand of spaghetti. Check the pasta occasionally as it cooks because the time given on packet instructions is often too long by a minute or two.

2. Meanwhile, heat the olive oil in a large saucepan and add the onion, garlic and chilli. Gently fry for about 8 minutes, or until the onion is soft. Add the anchovies and cook for another minute. Add the tomato, oregano, olive halves and capers and bring to the boil. Reduce the heat, season with salt and pepper, and leave the sauce to simmer for 3 minutes.

3. Drain the spaghetti and add it to the sauce. Toss together well so that the pasta is coated in the sauce. Scatter the basil over the top and serve.

After peeling the onion, take a little slice off its middle and stand the onion on this to stabilise it. Starting at one end, slice into rings until you are close to the middle, then move to the other end and slice back towards the middle. This will give you the steadiest hold for the longest time.

Prawn ravioli with basil butter

SERVES: 8 * PREPARATION TIME: 15 MINUTES * COOKING TIME: 5 MINUTES

Smaller ravioli are eaten in soups, while larger ones are served with butter or a simple sauce. The filling is usually meat but wild mushroom or squash are also popular. Ravioli are also known as agnolotti.

500 g (1 lb 2 oz) prawns (shrimp), peeled and deveined
1 tablespoon chopped chives
1 egg white, lightly beaten
330 ml (11¼ fl oz/1⅓ cups) cream
200 g (7 oz) packet gow gee wrappers (see Note) or fresh lasagne sheets, halved
1 egg, lightly beaten

Basil butter
125 g (4½ oz) butter
1 garlic clove, crushed
3 tablespoons finely shredded basil
40 g (1½ oz/¼ cup) pine nuts

1. Put the prawns in a food processor with the chives and egg white and process until smooth. Season with salt and pepper. Add the cream, being careful not to overprocess or the mixture will curdle.

2. Put 2-3 teaspoons of the prawn mixture in the centre of the gow gee wrappers (you won't need them all). Brush the edges with beaten egg, then fold over and press together to form semicircles. Press the edges to seal. Add in batches to a large pan of boiling water and cook each batch for 4 minutes. Drain, taking care not to damage the ravioli, and divide among warm serving plates.

3. For the basil butter, melt the butter gently in a pan, add the garlic and stir until fragrant. Add the shredded basil, pine nuts and a little freshly ground black pepper, and cook until the butter turns a nutty brown colour. Drizzle the butter over the ravioli. Serve immediately.

Note: Buy the gow gee wrappers from Asian food stores – they are thin, round or square wrappers made from wheat flour and water.

prawns

There many different types of prawn (gambero). Rather than judging by size, buy any that are fresh and in season—these will taste sweeter than frozen prawns, which are often woolly. Varieties of prawn are interchangeable in recipes: just ensure you have enough per person.

30 mins

Roast tomato risotto

SERVES: 4 ∗ **PREPARATION TIME: 5 MINUTES** ∗ **COOKING TIME: 25 MINUTES**

Tomatoes *(pomodori)* are almost synonymous with Italian cooking and are used as a main ingredient for many dishes. Surprisingly, they are not indigenous to the country and were brought from South America in the sixteenth century. They are available fresh, tinned, dried, puréed or roasted.

1 litre (35 fl oz/4 cups) chicken or
   vegetable stock
a pinch saffron threads
250 ml (9 fl oz/1 cup) dry white
   wine
2 tablespoons butter
1 onion, finely chopped
270 g (1⅓ cups) risotto rice
1 tablespoon olive oil
1 garlic clove, crushed
400 g (about 40) cherry tomatoes
parmesan cheese, grated
4 tablespoons parsley, finely
   chopped

1. Heat the stock in a saucepan until it is simmering, then leave it over a low heat. Put the saffron into the wine and leave it to soak.

2. Melt the butter in a large, deep, heavy-based frying pan, then gently cook the onion until it is soft, but not browned. Add the rice, turn the heat to low and stir well to coat all the grains of rice in the butter.

3. Add the wine and saffron to the rice, turn the heat up to medium and cook, stirring the rice, until all the liquid has been absorbed. Add 125 ml (4 fl oz/½ cup) stock, stirring constantly over medium heat until the liquid is absorbed. Continue adding more stock, 125 ml (4 fl oz/½ cup) at a time, stirring constantly for 20 minutes, or until all the stock is absorbed and the rice is tender and creamy.

4. While the rice is cooking, heat the oil in a saucepan, add the garlic and tomatoes, then fry for 2 to 3 minutes over medium heat until the tomatoes are slightly soft and have burst open. Season well.

5. Stir in 4 tablespoons of parmesan and the parsley. Spoon the tomatoes over the top and scatter with extra parmesan. Serve immediately.

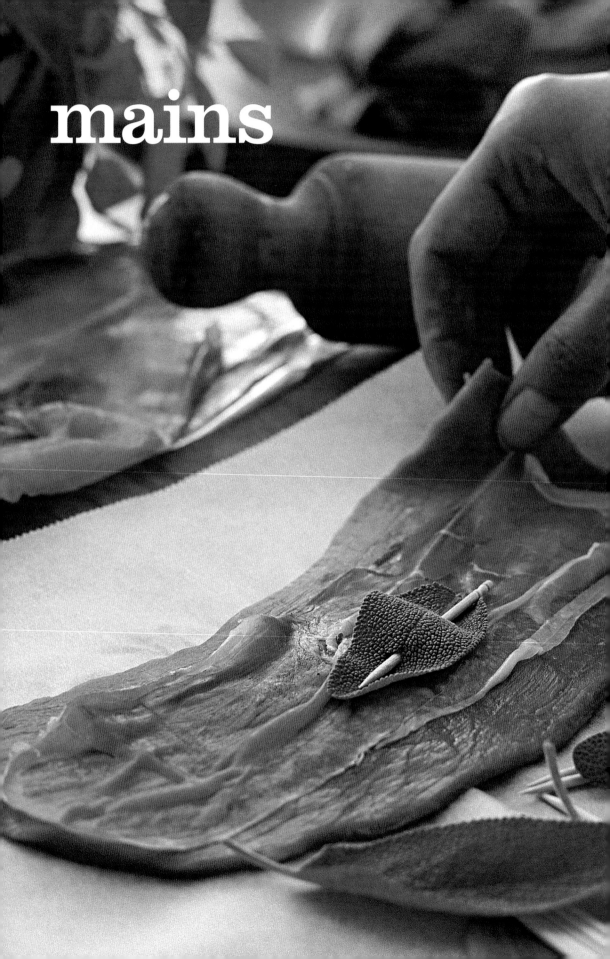

mains

The Italians are famed for the freshness of their ingredients: mushrooms and truffles are picked in the wild, herbs and vegetables carried swiftly from the ground to the plate. There are very few landlocked regions of Italy, the coastline is abundant with fresh seafood and even inland areas have a rich supply of freshwater fish in their rivers and streams. Anchovies, mussels, crabs and fish can be bought daily from bustling port markets and are usually simply prepared, plainly fried or grilled or made into a favourite local stew.

The Tuscans are known as the great meat-eaters of Italy, especially for beef. Pork is Italy's most commonly used meat, both fresh and cured into hams, salami, pancetta and sausages. For some simple meat dishes try the steak sandwich with salsa verde, the famous saltimbocca from Rome, or the Tuscan favourite of Italian sausages with white beans and gremolata.

The mainstay of Italian cooking, and certainly not seen as a mere accompaniment to meat or seafood, fresh vegetables are bought sometimes twice a day for lunch and dinner in local markets and chargrilled, grilled, fried, marinated or used for sauces, bakes and tossing through pasta. *Contorni* are vegetables served as side dishes with a meal. The frittata makes a fabulous vegetable main, and is both tasty and satisfying. Almost an omelette, but flashed under the grill to finish off the cooking, the frittata varies from thin and pancake-like, to thicker with a golden crust and creamy centre. For the winter try the cavolo nero and ricotta frittata and for the summer a perfect picnic addition is the frittata of courgette flowers, oregano and ricotta salata.

When Queen Margherita visited Naples and asked to sample the city's famed thin crisp bread with topping, called 'pizza', she gave royal endorsement to a humble idea that has now become one of the world's favourite foods.

30 mins

Mussels in chunky tomato sauce

SERVES: 6 ∗ **PREPARATION TIME: 10 MINUTES** ∗ **COOKING TIME: 20 MINUTES**

There are two main types of mussel *(cozze)* available: black or European mussels with their blueish black shells; and the green-lipped mussels of Southeast Asia, also called New Zealand mussels. Black mussels are smaller and generally have a better flavour; they are farmed and are usually sold cleaned and ready to cook.

1.5 kg (3 lb 5 oz) black mussels
1 tablespoon olive oil
1 large onion, diced
4 garlic cloves, finely chopped
800 g (1 lb 12 oz) tinned chopped
   tomatoes
3 tablespoons tomato purée
30 g (1 oz/¼ cup) pitted black
   olives
1 tablespoon capers, rinsed and
   squeezed dry
125 ml (4 fl oz/½ cup) fish stock
3 tablespoons chopped flat-leaf
   (Italian) parsley

1. Scrub the mussels with a stiff brush and pull out the hairy beards. Discard any damaged mussels, or any that don't close when tapped on the bench.

2. In a large saucepan, heat the olive oil and cook the onion and garlic over medium heat for 1-2 minutes, or until softened. Add the tomato, tomato purée, olives, capers and fish stock. Bring to the boil, then reduce the heat and simmer, stirring occasionally, for 15 minutes, or until the sauce is thick.

3. Stir in the mussels and cover the saucepan. Shake or toss the mussels occasionally and cook for 4-5 minutes, or until the mussels begin to open. Remove the pan from the heat and discard any mussels that haven't opened in the cooking time. Add the parsley, toss gently and serve.

Using a small sharp knife, remove any barnacles and pull away the hairy beard.

Tap open mussels on the work surface to close them. If they do not close discard them. Rinse well.

12 mins

Steak sandwich with salsa verde

SERVES: 4 ✳ **PREPARATION TIME: 10 MINUTES** ✳ **COOKING TIME: 2 MINUTES**

Salsa verde is a piquant sauce, full of flavour that marries perfectly with beef and also complements seafood, especially when barbecued.

2 garlic cloves, crushed
4 handfuls parsley
½ bunch basil leaves
½ bunch mint leaves
3 tablespoons olive oil
2 teaspoons capers, chopped
2 teaspoons lemon juice
2 teaspoons red wine vinegar
4 minute steaks
4 large pieces ciabatta or Turkish bread, halved horizontally
1 Lebanese (short) cucumber

1. To make the salsa verde, put the garlic and herbs in a food processor with 2 tablespoons of the oil and whiz them together until they are coarsely chopped. Tip the chopped herbs into a bowl and stir in the capers, lemon juice and vinegar. Season with salt and pepper.

2. Heat the remaining oil in a frying pan and fry the steaks for 1 minute on each side – they should cook very quickly and start to brown.

3. While the steaks are cooking, toast the bread. Spread some salsa verde on all the pieces of the bread and make four sandwiches with the steaks and cucumber.

You can mix the ingredients of the salsa verde by hand but ensure you blend in the olive oil slowly.

20 mins

Saltimbocca

SERVES: 4 ✳ PREPARATION TIME: 10 MINUTES ✳ COOKING TIME: 10 MINUTES

Saltimbocca, a dish that is usually associated with Rome, rather picturesquely translates as 'leap into your mouth'. Thin slices of veal are covered with a slice of prosciutto and a sage leaf. The veal can be left flat, or rolled up and secured with a cocktail stick.

8 small veal escalopes
8 slices prosciutto (dry-cured ham)
8 sage leaves
2 tablespoons olive oil
60 g (2¼ oz) butter
185 ml (6 fl oz/¾ cup) dry Marsala
    or dry white wine

1. Place the veal between two sheets of greaseproof paper and pound with a meat mallet or rolling pin until they are 5 mm (¼ inch) thick. Make sure you pound them evenly. Peel off the paper and season lightly. Cut the prosciutto slices to the same size as the veal. Cover each piece of veal with a slice of prosciutto and place a sage leaf in the centre. Secure the sage leaf with a cocktail stick.

2. Heat the olive oil and half the butter in a large frying pan. Add the veal in batches and fry, prosciutto side up, over medium heat for 3-4 minutes, or until the veal is just cooked through. Briefly flip the saltimbocca over and fry the prosciutto side. Transfer each batch to a warm plate as it is done.

3. Pour off the oil from the pan and add the Marsala or wine. Bring to the boil and cook over high heat until reduced by half, scraping up the bits from the bottom of the pan. Add the remaining butter and, when it has melted, season the sauce. Remove the cocktail sticks and spoon the sauce over the veal to serve.

Apply even pressure to avoid tearing.

Use cocktail sticks to attach the sage leaves.

Cavolo nero and ricotta frittata

SERVES: 4 * PREPARATION TIME: 10 MINUTES * COOKING TIME: 20 MINUTES

Cavolo nero is a type of cabbage and has a unique flavour, nuttier than regular cabbage, and can hold its own with stronger ingredients such as bacon, chilli and cheese. If it's not available, use dark green savoy cabbage instead.

150 g (5½ oz) cavolo nero
1 tablespoon olive oil
1 small onion, finely chopped
2 garlic cloves, crushed
200 g (7 oz) fresh ricotta cheese
6 eggs
½ teaspoon ground mace
2 tablespoons finely grated parmesan cheese
crusty bread or thick toast, to serve

1. Cut the leaves of the cavolo nero from the stems, wash and dry thoroughly, and roughly chop. Heat the oil in a 26 cm (10½ inch) non-stick frying pan, and cook the onion over medium heat for 3-4 minutes, or until soft. Add the garlic and cook for a further 1 minute.

2. Add half the cavolo nero to the pan, and toss until softened slightly, then add the remaining leaves and cook, stirring regularly, until soft and glossy dark green.

3. Beat the ricotta in a large bowl using electric beaters until smooth, then add the eggs and mace, and beat on low until combined. Don't worry if there are still a few little lumps of ricotta. Stir in the cavolo nero mixture and parmesan, and season with salt and freshly ground black pepper. Transfer the mixture back into the frying pan, and cook over medium-low heat for 8 minutes, or until set underneath.

4. Cook the top of the frittata under a hot grill (broiler) for 3-4 minutes, until set. (Test by pressing with a fork – the top may appear set but the centre may still be uncooked.) Turn out onto a plate and cut into eight wedges. Serve with crusty bread or thick toast.

ricotta

Ricotta means 'recooked'. It is a soft cheese made by recooking the whey left over from making other cheeses and draining it in baskets. It is produced as a by-product of many different types of cheese and varies in fat content. Hard, salted versions are available and there is also a ricotta made from buffalo milk. Fresh ricotta cut from a wheel has a better texture and flavour than that sold in tubs.

14 mins

Swordfish with anchovy and caper sauce

SERVES: 4 ∗ PREPARATION TIME: 10 MINUTES ∗ COOKING TIME: 4 MINUTES

Swordfish (pesce spada) are large fish, usually cut into steaks or sold as pieces of fillet. They are caught off the coast of Sicily and southern Italy, which is where they are eaten most. The flesh is paler than that of tuna and not quite so strongly flavoured.

Sauce
1 large garlic clove
1 tablespoon capers, rinsed and
  finely chopped
50 g (1¾ oz) anchovy fillets, finely
  chopped
1 tablespoon finely chopped
  rosemary or dried oregano
finely grated zest and juice of ½
  lemon
4 tablespoons extra virgin olive oil
1 large tomato, finely chopped

4 swordfish steaks
1 tablespoon extra virgin olive oil
crusty Italian bread, to serve

1. Put the garlic in a mortar and pestle with a little salt and crush it. To make the sauce, mix together the garlic, capers, anchovies, rosemary or oregano, lemon zest and juice, oil and tomato. Leave for 10 minutes.

2. Preheat a griddle or grill (broiler) to very hot. Using paper towels, pat the swordfish dry and lightly brush with the olive oil. Season with salt and pepper. Sear the swordfish over high heat for about 2 minutes on each side (depending on the thickness of the steaks), or until just cooked. The best way to check if the fish is cooked is to pull apart the centre of one steak – the flesh should be opaque. (Serve with the cut side underneath.)

3. If the cooked swordfish is a little oily, drain it on paper towels, then place on serving plates and drizzle with the sauce. Serve with Italian bread to mop up the sauce.

30 mins

Veal parmigiana

SERVES: 4 ✳ PREPARATION TIME: 15 MINUTES ✳ COOKING TIME: 15 MINUTES

Parmigiana is a deceptive name for this dish, as the recipe does not, in fact, hail from the city of Parma. Instead, its creation is claimed by almost every region of Italy, but the use of mozzarella and tomatoes indicates a dish from the south.

40 g (1½ oz/⅓ cup) plain (all-purpose) flour
2 eggs
65 g (2¼ oz/⅔ cup) dry breadcrumbs
2 teaspoons chopped oregano
4 large veal cutlets, well trimmed
1 tablespoon olive oil
ready-made tomato and garlic pasta sauce
100 g (3½ oz) mozzarella cheese, thinly sliced
35 g (1 oz/⅓ cup) grated parmesan cheese

1. Preheat the grill (broiler) to a high heat.

2. Meanwhile, place the flour in a wide shallow bowl and season well. Beat the eggs with 2 tablespoons of water in another bowl. Mix the breadcrumbs with the oregano, season and place in a third bowl.

3. Pound the cutlets between two sheets of plastic wrap until flattened to 5 mm (¼ inch) thick, taking care not to tear the flesh from the bone. Coat in the seasoned flour, shaking off the excess. Dip both sides in the egg mixture and then coat in the breadcrumbs. Heat olive oil in a large frying pan. Add the cutlets in two batches and brown over medium-high heat for 2 minutes on each side. Transfer to a shallow baking dish large enough to fit them side by side.

4. Spread the pasta sauce over each cutlet. Cover with the mozzarella and sprinkle with the parmesan. Bake under the grill (broiler) for 5-8 minutes, or until the cheeses have melted and browned. Serve.

veal

One of the most popular meats in Italy, veal (vitello) is used in many different ways. The cutlets, cut from the ribs, are dusted in flour or coated in crumbs and then fried. Scaloppine and picacata (thin slices cut from the rump or silverside) are used for dishes like saltimbocca. The shoulders and legs can be roasted whole or cubed for stew and ragùs and the loin used for vitello tonnato. Veal shanks (ossibuchi) are from the veal shins and cut into thick pieces. The bone has marrow in the centre and is surrounded by a thick piece of meat. Veal mince is also used for polpette.

25 mins

Bocconcini and semi-dried tomato pizza

SERVES: 4-6 * PREPARATION TIME: 10 MINUTES * COOKING TIME: 15 MINUTES

Bocconcini literally means 'small mouthful' and is used to describe various foods, but generally refers to small balls of mozzarella, about the size of walnuts.

1 large ready-made pizza base
3 tablespoons tomato pasta sauce
4 large bocconcini (fresh baby mozzarella cheese), sliced
120 g (4¼ oz) semi-dried (sun-blushed) tomatoes, drained
½ teaspoon sweet smoked paprika
25 g (1 oz/¼ cup) shaved Parmesan cheese
1 small handful baby basil leaves

1. Preheat the oven to 200°C (400°F/ Gas 6).

2. Lightly oil a 30 cm (12 inch) pizza pan. Place the ready-made pizza base in the prepared pan and spread the base with the pasta sauce. Arrange the bocconcini and tomatoes over the base and sprinkle with paprika. Bake in the oven for 15-20 minutes, or until golden and the base is crisp underneath.

3. Serve the pizza sprinkled with the parmesan and basil leaves.

Pork chops pizzaiola

SERVES: 4 * **PREPARATION TIME: 15 MINUTES** * **COOKING TIME: 15 MINUTES**

Pizzaiola sauce is a speciality of Naples. Its name is derived from its similarity to the tomato topping on that other speciality of the city: pizza. The sauce is versatile and can be served over beef, chicken or, as in this recipe, pork chops.

4 pork chops
4 tablespoons olive oil
600 g (1 lb 5 oz) ripe tomatoes
3 garlic cloves, crushed
3 basil leaves, torn into pieces
1 teaspoon finely chopped parsley,
   to serve

1. Using scissors or a knife, cut the pork fat at 5 mm (¼ inch) intervals around the rind. Brush the chops with 1 tablespoon of the olive oil and season well.

2. Remove the stems from the tomatoes and score a cross in the bottom of each one. Blanch in boiling water for 30 seconds. Transfer to cold water, peel the skin away from the cross and chop the tomatoes.

3. Heat 2 tablespoons of the oil in a saucepan over low heat and add the garlic. Soften without browning for 1-2 minutes, then add the tomato and season. Increase the heat, bring to the boil and cook for 5 minutes until thick. Stir in the basil.

4. Heat the remaining oil in a large frying pan with a tight-fitting lid. Brown the chops in batches over medium-high heat for 2 minutes on each side. Place in a slightly overlapping row down the centre of the pan and spoon the sauce over the top, covering the chops completely. Cover the pan and cook over low heat for about 5 minutes. Sprinkle with parsley to serve.

Snipping the fat at the edge of the pork chops will help them keep their shape. If the fat is left unsnipped, it shrinks faster than the meat as it cooks and makes the chops curl up at the edge.

30 mins

Baked tuna siciliana

**SERVES: 4 ∗ PREPARATION TIME: 10 MINUTES + MARINATING TIME
COOKING TIME: 20 MINUTES**

Tuna is caught off the coast of Sicily in huge tunnels of nets: a practice unique
to the region. Any dish called Siciliana usually means it is served with tomatoes
and anchovies.

80 ml (2½ fl oz/⅓ cup) olive oil
2 tablespoons lemon juice
2½ tablespoons finely chopped
 basil
4 x 175 g (6 oz) tuna steaks or
 swordfish steaks
60 g (2¼ oz) black olives, pitted
 and chopped
1 tablespoon baby capers, rinsed
 and patted dry
2 anchovies, finely chopped
400 g (14 oz) tomatoes, peeled,
 deseeded and chopped, or a 400 g
 (14 oz) tin chopped tomatoes
2 tablespoons dry breadcrumbs
bread for serving

1. Mix 2 tablespoons of the olive
oil with the lemon juice and 1
tablespoon of the basil. Season and
pour into a shallow, non-metallic
ovenproof dish, large enough to
hold the tuna steaks in a single layer.
Arrange the tuna in the dish and
leave to marinate until required.

2. Preheat the oven to 220°C
(425°F/ Gas 7) and preheat the
grill (broiler).

3. Combine the olives, capers,
anchovies and tomatoes with the
remaining oil and the remaining basil
and season well. Spread over the tuna
and sprinkle the breadcrumbs over
the top. Bake for about 15 minutes, or
until the fish is just opaque. Finish off by
placing briefly under the hot grill until
the breadcrumbs are crisp. Serve with
bread to soak up the juices.

tinned tomatoes

Tinned peeled tomatoes
have been used in Italy
since the end of the
eighteenth century. The
best brand for tinning
are San Marzano plum
tomatoes and it is these
that are sold worldwide
as Italian tinned
tomatoes. It is perfectly
acceptable to use tinned
tomatoes for recipes such
as sauces—they are of
uniform ripeness and are
already peeled for ease of
preparation. You may need
to add a pinch of sugar to
counteract their acidity.

25 mins

Frittata of courgette flowers, oregano and ricotta salata

SERVES: 4 ✳ **PREPARATION TIME: 10 MINUTES** ✳ **COOKING TIME: 15 MINUTES**

Originating in Sicily, ricotta salata is a firm white rindless cheese with a nutty, sweet milky flavour. If unavailable, substitute with a mild feta cheese.

2 tablespoons olive oil
1 onion, finely chopped
2 garlic cloves, finely sliced
8 small courgettes (zucchini) with flowers
8 eggs, lightly whisked
7 g (1¼ oz/¼ cup) oregano, chopped
35 g (1¼ oz/⅓ cup) ricotta salata, grated
25 g (1 oz/¼ cup) grated parmesan cheese
1 tablespoon shave parmesan cheese
lemon wedges, to serve

1. Preheat the oven to 200°C (400°F/ Gas 6). Heat the oil in an ovenproof 20 cm (8 inch) frying pan and cook the onion and garlic until softened. Arrange the courgette flowers evenly in the pan, and add the egg. Sprinkle the oregano, ricotta salata and grated parmesan over the top and season well with black pepper.

2. Put the pan in the oven and cook for about 10 minutes, or until set. Remove from the oven and allow to cool slightly. Top with the shaved parmesan, cut into wedges and serve with a piece of lemon.

oregano

A popular herb, especially in the south of Italy, oregano (origano) is used both fresh and dried, but is much more commonly seen dried. It goes well with tomato sauces and other stronger-tasting vegetables and is often used when roasting meats.

25 mins

Italian sausage with white beans and gremolata

SERVES: 4 ✳ **PREPARATION TIME: 10 MINUTES** ✳ **COOKING TIME: 15 MINUTES**

Salsiccia is the general name in Italy for sausages. It is traditionally made with ground pork, pork fat, spices and herbs, though some varieties are made with other meats.

3 tablespoons (¼ cup) olive oil
12 Italian sausages or thick pork
  sausages, cut into chunks
6 garlic cloves, peeled and smashed
240 g (9 oz) chargrilled red or
  yellow pepper (capsicum)
2 x 400 g (14 oz) tins cannellini
  beans, drained and rinsed
1½ tablespoons grated lemon zest
2 large handfuls parsley, chopped
2 tablespoons lemon juice
extra virgin olive oil, for drizzling

1. Heat the olive oil in a frying pan and cook the sausages until they are browned all over and cooked through. Lift them out of the frying pan with a slotted spoon and put them to one side.

2. Put 3 garlic cloves in the frying pan and cook them over gentle heat until they are very soft. Cut the pepper into strips and add them to the pan, along with the beans and sausages. Stir together and cook over a gentle heat for 2 minutes to heat the sausages through. Season well with salt and pepper.

3. To make the gremolata, smash the remaining 3 garlic cloves to a paste, with a little salt, in a mortar and pestle. Mix in the lemon zest and the chopped parsley and season with salt and pepper.

4. Just before serving, stir the gremolata through the beans and then finish the dish with the lemon juice and a drizzle of olive oil.

30 mins

Turkey spiedini

SERVES: 4 ✴ **PREPARATION TIME: 15 MINUTES** ✴ **COOKING TIME: 15 MINUTES**

The trick to making skewers *(spiedini)* is to ensure all the ingredients are cut to the same size so they cook evenly. This recipe uses slices of lemon, but if you want a stronger flavour you can use the lemon zest and pith instead. Pork, veal or chicken mince can be used instead of turkey.

1 teaspoon fennel seeds
1 garlic clove
400 g (14 oz) minced turkey
2 tablespoons chopped oregano,
   marjoram or thyme
1 large lemon
1 thick slice of bread, crust
   removed, cut into 2 cm (1¾ inch)
   cubes
8 bay leaves
1 tablespoon olive oil

4 metal or wooden kebab skewers
   or sticks

1. Put the fennel seeds and garlic in a mortar and pestle and crush with a pinch of salt. If you don't have a mortar and pestle, crush them in a small bowl with the end of a rolling pin or in a spice grinder.

2. Mix the fennel and garlic with the turkey mince and herbs and season with pepper. Test the seasoning by frying a teaspoon of the mixture in a little oil and tasting for flavour.

3. Peel the lemon completely, removing the zest and white pith. Cut the lemon into four thick slices, then cut the slices in half, making eight pieces (for a stronger flavour, use the lemon zest instead of the flesh). Roll the turkey mince into 16 small balls, pressing firmly so they won't break up when cooked.

4. To assemble a kebab, start with a piece of bread, spear it onto the skewer and push it to the end. Next, push on a ball of turkey and shape it to the thickness of the bread. Next, place a slice of lemon, followed by a turkey ball, a bay leaf, a piece of bread, a turkey ball, lemon slice, turkey ball, bay leaf and finish with a piece of bread. Put the kebabs on a plate and drizzle with olive oil (mostly over the bread so that it soaks up some of the oil).

5. Heat a griddle or grill to very hot, then reduce the heat to medium. Season the kebabs and cook for about 15 minutes, turning once. Check that the heat is not too high – the kebabs need to brown and cook through rather than burn on the outside. Squeeze a little lemon juice over the top before serving.

20 mins

Veal marsala

SERVES: 4 * **PREPARATION TIME: 10 MINUTES** * **COOKING TIME: 10 MINUTES**

A fortified wine from Marsala in Sicily that comes in varying degrees of dryness and sweetness, dry Marsalas are used in savoury dishes such as risotto, and sweet ones in desserts such as zabaglione. Do not try to use sweet Marsala in savoury dishes.

4 pieces (500 g/ 1lb 2oz) veal schnitzel
plain (all-purpose) flour, seasoned
50g (1¾ oz) butter
1 tablespoon oil
185 ml (6 fl oz/¾ cup) dry Marsala
3 teaspoons cream
30g (1oz) butter, chopped, extra

1. Using a meat mallet or the heel of your hand, flatten the schnitzel pieces to 5 mm (¼ inch) thick. Dust the veal in the flour, shaking off any excess. Heat the butter and oil in a large frying pan and cook the veal over medium-high heat for 1-2 minutes on each side, or until almost cooked through. Remove and keep warm.

2. Add the Marsala to the pan and bring to the boil, scraping the base of the pan to loosen any sediment. Reduce the heat and simmer for 1-2 minutes, or until slightly reduced. Add the cream and simmer for 2 minutes, then whisk in the extra butter until the sauce thickens slightly. Return the veal to the pan and simmer for 1 minute, or until the meat is warmed through. Serve immediately.

Note: Purchase veal that is pale in colour and free of sinew. Sinew will make the meat tough.

Barbecued squid with picada dressing

SERVES: 4 ＊ PREPARATION TIME: 10 MINUTES ＊ COOKING TIME: 5 MINUTES

The general rule when cooking squid and octopus is to do so either very briefly or for a very long time — anything in the middle tends to result in tough meat. When buying squid, ready-cleaned squid tubes are the easiest option. Scoring a criss-cross pattern on the inner surface of squid tubes causes them to curl up into attractive pinecone-like shapes, or flowers, when cooked.

750 g (1 lb 10 oz) small squid, cleaned
rocket (arugula) leaves, for serving
crusty bread, for serving

Picada dressing
60 ml (2 fl oz/¼ cup) extra virgin olive oil
3 tablespoons finely chopped flat-leaf (Italian) parsley
2 garlic cloves, crushed

Fish substitution
cuttlefish, octopus, prawns (shrimp), or even chunks of firm white fish fillet

1. Wash the squid tubes and tentacles and drain well. Place in a bowl, add ¼ teaspoon salt and mix well. Heat a lightly oiled barbecue flatplate or chargrill pan over medium-high heat.

2. For the picada dressing, whisk together the olive oil, parsley, garlic, ½ teaspoon freshly ground black pepper and some salt in a small jug or bowl.

3. Cook the squid in small batches on the barbecue or in a chargrill pan for about 2-3 minutes, or until the tubes are white and tender. Barbecue or chargrill the squid tentacles, turning to brown them all over for 1 minute, or until they curl up. Serve hot, drizzled with the picada dressing, with rocket leaves and crusty bread.

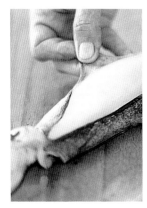

Clean the squid by first pulling off the skin and wings.

Use a spoon to clean inside the squid.

20 mins

Pizzette

SERVES: 4 * **PREPARATION TIME: 5 MINUTES** * **COOKING TIME: 15 MINUTES**

Pizza first existed as a bread to accompany meals. The original topping for a pizza bianca (white pizza) was garlic, lard, salt and anchovies. The true Neapolitan pizza has a thin crust and is baked on the floor of a very hot wood-fired oven for 1-2 minutes.

4 x ready-made mini pizza bases
2 tablespoons tomato purée (paste)
1 garlic clove, crushed
1 teaspoon dried oregano
20 g (½ oz) lean shaved ham
2 teaspoons grated light mozzarella cheese
chopped rocket (arugula), to serve
extra virgin olive oil, to serve

1. Preheat the oven to 200°C (400°F/ Gas 6). Place pizza bases on a baking tray.

2. Combine the tomato purée, garlic, oregano and 1 tablespoon water. Spread the paste over each base then top with the ham and mozzarella. Bake for 12-15 minutes, or until crisp and golden on the edges. Just before serving, top with chopped rocket and drizzle with extra virgin olive oil.

desserts

Italians adore their dessert course *(dolci)*, and love to indulge, without guilt, in the creamy, rich confections for which their dessert repertoire is so famed. Although some recipes in this chapter require additional standing, cooling or refrigeration to reach perfection, the beauty with so many Italian dessert recipes is that they are quick and easy to create and can be prepared in advance.

The Arabs brought sugar to Sicily and the southern island is now the sweet-producing heart of the country: gelati, sorbets and granita are sold in cafés and at the roadside in an awe-inspiring array of colours and flavours. This chapter includes a number of superb recipes showcasing these frozen delights, like almond semifreddo and chocolate affogato. But Italy is renowned for more than its ices: the tiramisu of Treviso, the dome-shaped zuccotto of Florence and, of course simple poached or grilled fruits are all perfect Italian endings to a meal.

Ricotta is a popular ingredient used in Italian desserts. Produced as a by-product of cheese-making, ricotta is a fresh, slightly sweet cheese created by skimming off the milk solids left in the whey. It is low in fat, has a delicate light texture and is a versatile ingredient in both sweet and savoury dishes.

Desserts featuring sponge cake are also very popular in Italy, as can be seen in the famous tiramisu, zuccotto, zuppa inglese and cassata. If you are short on time, buy a madeira (pound) cake or even a pandoro instead. Each will work equally well.

It is important, when deciding which dessert to serve, to consider what has come before it and balance flavours, richness and textures with previous courses. For example, avoid serving a cream-based dessert such as tiramisu if a dairy-rich main course has been on the menu. Similarly, if the main course has been a hearty dish, make the dessert a fruit-based one, or at least something very light. If you really want to indulge in a memorably rich dessert, then serve a simple grill (fish or chicken, perhaps) or even a main-course salad, before doing so.

Tiramisu

SERVES: 4 ✳ PREPARATION TIME: 20 MINUTES ✳ COOKING TIME: NIL

Tiramisu means 'pick me up' in Italian – a reference, no doubt, to the generous shot of brandy in this rich dessert. It was created in the 1960s in a Treviso restaurant and has rapidly become popular in many other countries.

5 eggs, separated
180 g (6 oz) caster (superfine) sugar
250 g (9 oz) mascarpone cheese
250 ml (9 fl oz/1 cup) cold very strong coffee
3 tablespoons brandy or sweet Marsala
44 small sponge finger biscuits
80 g (2¾ oz) dark chocolate, finely grated

1. Beat the egg yolks with the sugar until the sugar has dissolved and the mixture is light and fluffy and leaves a ribbon trail when dropped from the whisk. Add the mascarpone and beat until the mixture is smooth. Whisk the egg whites in a clean dry glass bowl until soft peaks form. Fold into the mascarpone mixture.

2. Pour the coffee into a shallow dish and add the brandy. Dip some of the sponge finger biscuits into the coffee mixture, using enough biscuits to cover the base of a 25 cm (10 inch) square dish. The biscuits should be fairly well soaked on both sides but not so much so that they break up. Arrange the biscuits in one tightly packed layer in the base of the dish.

3. Spread half the mascarpone mixture over the layer of biscuits. Add another layer of soaked biscuits and then another layer of mascapone, smoothing the top layer neatly. Leave to rest in the fridge for 10-15 minutes or until required. Dust with the grated chocolate to serve.

mascarpone
A cream cheese originally from Lombardy. Made with cream rather than milk, it is very high in fat. Mascarpone is generally used in desserts such as tiramisu or instead of cream in sauces. Widely available, it is usually sold in tubs.

15 mins

Panna cotta

SERVES: 4 ∗ **PREPARATION TIME: 10 MINUTES** ∗ **COOKING TIME: 5 MINUTES**

Meaning 'cooked cream', panna cotta is a rich creamy dessert set with leaf or powdered gelatine. Generally, gelatine leaves will give better results, although they may be harder to find. Whichever you choose, take care to use the amount specified or your panna cotta may end up rubbery.

450 ml (16 fl oz) thick (double/ heavy) cream
4 tablespoons caster (superfine) sugar
2 tablespoons grappa (optional)
vanilla extract
3 leaves or 1¼ teaspoons gelatine
250 g (9 oz) berries, to serve

1. Put the cream and sugar in a saucepan and stir over gentle heat until the sugar has dissolved. Bring to the boil, then simmer for 3 minutes, adding the grappa and a few drops of vanilla extract to taste.

2. If you are using the gelatine leaves, soak them in cold water until floppy, then squeeze out any excess water. Stir the leaves into the hot cream until they are completely dissolved. If you are using powdered gelatine, sprinkle it onto the hot cream in an even layer and leave it to absorb for a minute, then stir it into the cream until dissolved.

3. Pour the mixture into four 125 ml (4 fl oz/½ cup) metal or ceramic ramekins, cover each with a piece of plastic wrap and refrigerate until set.

4. Unmould the panna cotta by placing the ramekins very briefly in a bowl of hot water and then tipping them gently onto plates. Metal ramekins will take a shorter time than ceramic to unmould as they heat up quickly. Serve with the fresh berries.

grappa

This grape-based spirit is made from the crushed fruit used for wine-making. Grappa is usually drunk at room temperature after a meal as a digestive, but it can also be added to dishes such as zuppa inglese.

25 mins

Baked apples

SERVES: 6 * **PREPARATION TIME: 5 MINUTES** * **COOKING TIME: 25 MINUTES**

The advantage of this simple but elegant dessert is that the apples can be prepared and baked in advance and then gently warmed through just before serving. Take care not to overcook the apples or they will collapse. Serve with ice cream or crème fraîche.

6 cooking apples
75 g (2½ oz) unsalted butter, chilled
6 small cinnamon sticks
100 g (3½ oz/⅔ cup) pistachio nuts or pine nuts
3 tablespoons brown sugar
100 g (3½ oz/¾ cup) raisins or sultanas
200 ml (7 fl oz) grappa

1. Preheat the oven to 200°C (400°F/Gas 6). Remove the cores from the apples with a sharp knife or corer and put the cored apples in an ovenproof dish.

2. Divide the butter into six sticks and push one stick into the cores of each apple. Push a cinnamon stick into the middle of each apple and scatter with the nuts, sugar and raisins. Finally, pour over the grappa.

3. Bake for 20-25 minutes, basting the apples occasionally with the juices in the dish until they are soft when tested with a skewer.

Almond semifreddo

SERVES: 8-10 ∗ **PREPARATION TIME: 5 MINUTES + FREEZING TIME 1 HOUR**
COOKING TIME: NIL

Semifreddo means semi-frozen, so if you want to leave it in the freezer overnight, remove it and place it in the refrigerator for 30 minutes to soften slightly before serving.

**500 ml (17 fl oz) tub premium
  vanilla ice cream, softened**
60 ml (2 fl oz/¼ cup) amaretto
**80 g (2¾ oz/½ cup) blanched
  almonds, toasted and chopped**
8 amaretti biscuits crushed

fresh fruit or extra Amaretto

1. Line a 10 x 21 cm (4 x 8¼ inch) loaf tin with plastic wrap so that it overhangs the two long sides.

2. Place the softened ice cream in a medium glass bowl. Stir the Amaretto, almonds and amaretti biscuits into the ice cream. Carefully spoon the mixture into the lined loaf tin and cover with the overhanging plastic. Freeze for 1 hour, or until frozen but not rock hard. Serve in slices with fresh fruit or a sprinkling of Amaretto. The semifreddo can also be poured into individual moulds or serving dishes before freezing.

amaretto

This sweet bitter-almond liqueur is drunk as a digestif after a meal, but you will also find it used in many sweet recipes as a flavouring.

30 mins

Individual zuccotto

SERVES: 6 * **PREPARATION TIME: 15 MINUTES + REFRIGERATION**
COOKING TIME: NIL

Zuccotto is a traditional Florentine dessert, its shape inspired by the rounded roof of the local duomo. It consists of a sponge filled with layers of chocolate, mascarpone, fruit (traditionally candied fruit) and nuts. You can use a ready-made madeira (pound) or sponge cake to save time.

450 g packet madeira cake
60 ml (2 fl oz/¼ cup) Cointreau
60 ml (2 fl oz/¼ cup) brandy
300 ml (10½ fl oz) thick (double) cream
3 teaspoons icing (confectioner's) sugar, sifted
80 g (½ cup) blanched almonds, roasted, roughly chopped
70 g (5½ oz/½ cup) hazelnuts, roasted, roughly chopped
150 g good-quality dark chocolate, finely chopped

1. Cut the cake into 5 mm (¼ inch) slices. Lightly grease six 150 ml (5 fl oz) ramekins and line with plastic, leaving enough to hang over the sides. Press the pieces of the cake into the ramekins, overlapping to cover the base and sides. Combine the Cointreau and brandy in a bowl. Brush the cake with half the Cointreau mixture.

2. Place the cream and icing sugar in a bowl, and, using electric beaters, beat until firm and stiff. Fold in the nuts, chocolate and 1½ teaspoons Cointreau mixture. The mixture will be quite stiff.

3. Spoon the mixture into each ramekin and smooth over the surface. Cover with the overhanging plastic wrap and refrigerate for 15 minutes or longer if necessary. To serve, use the plastic wrap to lift the zuccotto out of the ramekins, turn upside-down onto serving plates and brush with the remaining Cointreau mixture.

30 mins

Amaretti-stuffed peaches

SERVES: 6 ✳ **PREPARATION TIME: 10 MINUTES** ✳ **COOKING TIME: 20 MINUTES**

Amaretti are small biscuits like macaroons, made from sweet and bitter almonds. Amaretti vary in size, but are usually 2-3 cm wide. They often come in pairs, wrapped in pieces of coloured paper like giant sweets.

6 ripe peaches
60 g (2¼ oz) amaretti biscuits, crushed
1 egg yolk
2 tablespoons caster (superfine) sugar
20 g (¾ oz/¼ cup) ground almonds
1 tablespoon amaretto
60 ml (2 fl oz/¼ cup) white wine
1 teaspoon caster sugar, extra
20 g (¾ oz) unsalted butter

1. Preheat the oven to 180°C (350°F/ Gas 4) and lightly grease a 30 x 25 cm ovenproof dish with butter.

2. Cut each peach in half and carefully remove the stones. Scoop a little of the pulp out from each and combine in a small bowl with the crushed biscuits, egg yolk, caster sugar, ground almonds and amaretto.

3. Spoon some of the mixture into each peach and place them cut-side-up in the dish. Sprinkle with the white wine and the extra sugar. Put a dot of butter on top of each and bake for 20 minutes, or until golden.

Note: When they are in season, you can also use ripe apricots or nectarines for this recipe. Allow three apricots/nectarines per person.

Chocolate affogato

SERVES: 4 * **PREPARATION TIME: 5 MINUTES** * **COOKING TIME: NIL**

Affogato literally means 'poached' or 'drowned'. Here it refers to the scoop of chocolate ice cream with a shot of liqueur poured over it that is then 'drowned' in a cup of hot espresso. This is served both as a coffee and a dessert.

500 ml tub premium chocolate
ice cream
4 small cups of espresso or very
strong coffee
4 shots Frangelico or any other
liqueur that you like

1. Scoop four balls of ice cream out of the container and put them into four cups, then put these in the freezer while you make the coffee.

2. Serve the ice cream with the Frangelico and coffee poured over it.

espresso

An espresso is made from a small quantity of coffee through which water is forced under pressure. This produces a dark rich coffee topped with an orange-brown crema (foam).

Zuppa inglese

SERVES: 6 * PREPARATION TIME: 10 MINUTES * COOKING TIME: 10 MINUTES

The name of this, which is similar in construction to the English trifle, does not literally translate to 'English soup', as might be assumed. The zuppa has the same linguistic background as the English 'sops' and refers to bread (or, in this case, cake) soaked in wine.

Custard
6 large egg yolks
100 g (3½ oz/½ cup) caster (superfine) sugar
2 tablespoons cornflour
1 tablespoon plain (all purpose) flour
600 ml (21 fl oz/2½ cups) milk
½ vanilla bean or 1 teaspoon vanilla extract

1 ready-made sponge cake
150 ml (5 fl oz/⅔ cup) clear alcohol, such as grappa or kirsch
200 g (7 oz/1⅔ cups) raspberries
350 g (12 oz/3 cups) blackberries
2 teaspoons caster sugar
250 ml (9 fl oz/1 cup) whipping cream

1. To make the custard, whisk the egg yolks with the sugar until pale and fluffy. Add the cornflour and flour and mix well. Heat the milk with the vanilla bean and bring just to the boil. Pour into the egg mixture, whisking as you do so. Pour back into the saucepan and gently bring to the boil, stirring all the time. Once the mixture is just boiling, take it off the heat and stir for another few minutes. Pour into a bowl and cover the surface with plastic wrap to prevent a skin forming.

2. Slice the sponge into 2 cm (¾ inch) strips. Place a couple of pieces on each plate (you need to use deep plates) and brush with about 100 ml (3½ fl oz) of the alcohol. Leave to soak for at least 10 minutes.

3. Put the raspberries and blackberries in a saucepan with the remaining alcohol and the caster sugar. Gently warm through so that the sugar just melts, then set aside to cool. Spoon over the sponge, then pour the custard over the top of the fruit. Lightly whip the cream and serve on the side.

When you heat milk, make sure that you use a heavy-based saucepan. The protein in milk coagulates and burns very easily, so keep stirring as it comes to the boil. Stirring will also prevent a skin forming— once a skin has formed, it cannot be stirred back into the milk.

Panforte

MAKES: 1 X 20 CM CAKE ✳ **PREPARATION TIME: 5 MINUTES** ✳ **COOKING TIME: 25 MINUTES**

Panforte is a medieval recipe from the twelfth or thirteenth century, a speciality of Siena where nearly every shop seems to feature it. This rich cake is sold in huge wheels of both blonde and dark panforte (the latter made by adding cocoa) and will keep for about 2 weeks.

4 small sheets rice paper
100 g (3½ oz/¾ cup) roasted
　hazelnuts
100 g (3½ oz/⅔ cup) roasted
　almonds
1 teaspoon each whole coriander
　seeds, cloves, nutmeg and black
　peppercorns
1 teaspoon ground cinnamon
50 g (1¾ oz/¼ cup) finely chopped
　dried figs
1 tablespoon cocoa
200 g (7 oz) roughly chopped
　candied or ange and lemon peel
grated zest of 1 lemon
50 g plain (all purpose) flour
150 g (5½ oz) sugar
4 tablespoons clear honey
2 tablespoons unsalted butter
icing (confectioner's) sugar, to dust

1. Butter and line the base of a 20 cm (8 inch) springform tin with rice paper. Cut a few thin strips to line the side as well. Preheat the oven to 150° (300°F/ Gas 3).

2. Grind the whole spices together in a spice grinder or mortar and pestle. Put the nuts in a metal or china bowl with the spices, figs, cocoa, candied peel, lemon zest and flour and mix.

3. Put the sugar, honey and butter in a heavy-based saucepan to melt, briefly stirring the butter into the sugar as it just starts to melt. Do not stir again or the sugar will crystallise. Bring to the boil and cook until the syrup reaches 120° (245°F) on a sugar thermometer, or a little of it dropped into cold water forms a soft ball when moulded between your finger and thumb.

4. Immediately pour the syrup into the nut mixture and mix well, working quickly as it will soon cool and stiffen. Pour into the tin and smooth the top with a spatula.

5. Bake for about 15 minutes. Unlike other cakes, this will not colour or seem very firm, even when cooked, but will begin to harden as it cools. Allow to cool a little in the tin until it is firm enough to enable the side of the tin to be removed. If the mixture is still quite soft when cooled, place in the fridge to set. To serve, dust the top heavily with icing sugar.

The cake is so sticky that you must use an edible paper.

If the mixture cools too quickly warm it up again in a microwave.

30 mins

Zabaglione

SERVES: 4 ＊ **PREPARATION TIME: 10 MINUTES + REFRIGERATION**
COOKING TIME: 10 MINUTES

Zabaglione (zabaione) is one of the lucky accidents of the culinary world. It came into being in the seventeenth century when a chef in the court of Savoy mistakenly poured sweet wine into an egg custard. Today it is eaten on its own or served as a sauce over fruit, cake or pastries.

6 egg yolks
3 tablespoons caster (superfine) sugar
125 ml (4 fl oz/½ cup) sweet Marsala
250 ml (9 fl oz/1 cup) double (thick/heavy) cream

1. Whisk the egg yolks and sugar in the top of a double boiler or in a heatproof bowl set over a saucepan of simmering water. Make sure that the base of the bowl does not touch the water or the egg may overcook and stick. It is important that you whisk constantly to move the cooked mixture from the outside of the bowl to the centre.

2. When the mixture is tepid, add the Marsala and whisk for another 5 minutes, or until it has thickened enough to hold its shape when drizzled off the whisk into the bowl.

3. Whip the cream until soft peaks form. Gently fold in the egg yolk and Marsala mixture. Divide among four glasses or bowls. Cover and refrigerate for 10-15 minutes or until required.

Before heating, the mixture is dark yellow and thin.

The zabaglione is ready when it holds its shape.

25 mins

Grilled figs with ricotta

SERVES: 4 ✳ **PREPARATION TIME: 10 MINUTES** ✳ **COOKING TIME: 15 MINUTES**

Originally from Syria, figs are now grown in many areas of Italy, including Puglia, Calabria and Sicily. They are a versatile fruit – they can be eaten fresh with Parma ham, their soft, sweet flesh can be minced and used in cakes, or they can be baked until soft and golden, as here.

2 tablespoons honey
1 cinnamon stick
3 tablespoons flaked almonds
4 large (or 8 small) fresh figs
125 g (4½ oz/½ cup) ricotta cheese
½ teaspoon vanilla essence
2 tablespoons icing (confectioner's)
  sugar, sifted
pinch ground cinnamon
½ teaspoon finely grated orange
  zest

1. Place the honey and cinnamon stick in a small saucepan with 80 ml (2½ fl oz/⅓ cup) water. Bring to the boil, then reduce the heat and simmer gently for 6 minutes, or until thickened and reduced by half. Discard the cinnamon stick and stir in the almonds.

2. Preheat the grill to moderately hot and grease a shallow ovenproof dish large enough to fit all the figs side by side. Slice the figs into quarters from the top to within 1cm of the bottom, keeping them attached at the base. Arrange in the prepared dish.

3. Combine the ricotta, vanilla, icing sugar, ground cinnamon and orange zest in a small bowl. Divide the filling among the figs, spooning it into their cavities. Spoon the syrup over the top. Place under the grill and cook until the juices start to come out from the figs and the almonds are lightly toasted. Cool for 2-3 minutes. Spoon the juices and any fallen almonds from the bottom of the dish over the figs and serve.

Cassata

SERVES: 10-12 * PREPARATION TIME: 30 MINUTES + FREEZING * COOKING TIME: NIL

There are two different dishes named cassata, one a cake made with ricotta and candied fruit, the other an ice-cream dessert. This cassata in its cake form is a classic Sicilian dish decorated with brightly coloured icings, marzipan and candied fruit.

1 ready-made sponge cake
4 tablespoons sweet Marsala
350 g (12 oz/1⅓ cup) ricotta cheese
75 g caster (superfine) sugar
½ teaspoon vanilla extract
100 g (3½ oz/ ½ cup) mixed candied fruit (orange, lemon, cherries, pineapple, apricot), finely chopped
50 g (1¾ oz) dark chocolate, chopped
green food colouring
250 g (9 oz) marzipan
2 tablespoons apricot or strawberry jam
100 g (3½ oz) icing (confectioner's) sugar

1. Use plastic wrap to line a 20 cm (7 ¾ inch) round cake tin with sloping sides (a moule à manqué would be perfect). Cut the cake into 5mm (¼ inch) slices to line the tin, reserving enough pieces to cover the top. Fit the slices of cake carefully into the tin, making sure there are no gaps. Brush the Marsala over the cake in the tin, as evenly as possible and reserving a little for the top.

2. Put the ricotta in a bowl and beat until smooth. Add the sugar and vanilla extract and mix well. Mix in the candied fruit and chocolate. Spoon the mixture into the mould, smooth the surface and then cover with the remaining slices of cake. Cover with plastic wrap and press the top down hard. Put the cassata in the freezer for 15 minutes, then unmould onto a plate.

3. Meanwhile knead enough green food colouring into the marzipan to tint it light green. Roll out the marzipan in a circle until it is large enough to completely cover the top and side of the cassata. Melt the jam in a saucepan with 1 tablespoon of water and brush over the cassata. Position the marzipan over the top and trim it to fit around the edge.

4. Mix the icing sugar with a little hot water to make a smooth icing that will spread easily. Either pipe the icing onto the cassata in a decorative pattern, or drizzle it over the top in a crosshatch pattern. Serve immediately.

Line the tin carefully leaving no gaps.

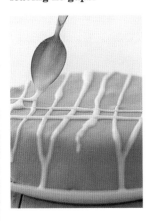

A crosshatch pattern looks neatest.

Fruit poached in red wine

SERVES: 6 * **PREPARATION TIME: 10 MINUTES** * **COOKING TIME: 20 MINUTES**

When poaching fruit, it is best to use varieties that hold their shape when cooked instead of breaking down to a soft mush. Good apples for poaching include granny smiths, braeburns, cox's, russets or pink ladies. Good cooking pears include conference, beurre bosc and anjou.

3 pears, quartered and cored

3 apples, peeled, quartered and cored

50 g (1¾ oz) sugar

1 vanilla pod, cut in half lengthways

2 small cinnamon sticks

400 ml (14 fl oz) red wine

200 ml (7 fl oz) dessert wine or port

700 g (1 lb 9 oz) red-skinned plums, halved

1. Put the pears and apples in a large saucepan. Add the sugar, vanilla pod, cinnamon sticks, red wine and dessert wine and bring to the boil. Reduce the heat and gently simmer for about 5-10 minutes, or until just soft.

2. Add the plums, stirring them through the pears and apples, and bring the liquid back to a simmer. Cook for another 5 minutes or until the plums are soft.

3. Remove the saucepan from the heat, cover with a lid and leave the fruit to marinate in the syrup until required. Reheat gently to serve warm or serve at room temperature with cream or ice cream and a biscuit.

Make sure that you cook the fruit at a gentle simmer. If it cooks too fast, the pieces will break up.

index

A READER'S DIGEST BOOK

Published by The Reader's Digest Association Limited
11 Westferry Circus
Canary Wharf
London E14 4HE
www.readersdigest.co.uk

We are committed both to the quality of our products and the service we
provide to our customers. We value your comments, so please do call us on
08705 113366, or via our website at www.readersdigest.co.uk. If you have any
comments about the content of any of our books, you can contact us at
gbeditorial@readersdigest.co.uk

Copyright © 2008 Murdoch Books Pty Limited

This book was designed, edited and produced by Murdoch Books Pty Limited.

Series Food Editor: Fiona Roberts
Designer: Joanna Byrne
Design Concept: Uber Creative
Production: Elizabeth Malcolm

PRINTED IN CHINA.

IMPORTANT: Those who might be at risk from the effects of salmonella
poisoning (the elderly, pregnant women, young children and those suffering
from immune deficiency diseases) should consult their doctor with any
concerns about eating raw eggs.

CONVERSION GUIDE: You may find cooking times vary depending on the
oven you are using. For fan-assisted ovens, as a general rule, set the oven
temperature to 20°C (35°F) lower than indicated in the recipe.

Book code: 410-716 UP0000-1
ISBN: 978 0 276 44 265 0
Oracle code: 250011998H